CANADA AND THE EUROPEAN COMMUNITY:
An Uncomfortable Partnership?

CANADA AND THE EUROPEAN COMMUNITY:
An Uncomfortable Partnership?

N. G. PAPADOPOULOS

The Institute for Research on Public Policy
L'Institut de recherches politiques

Legal Deposit Third Quarter
Bibliothèque nationale du Québec

Canadian Cataloguing in Publication Data

Papadopoulos, N.G. (Nicolas G.), 1946-
Canada and the European Community

(Essays in international economics, ISSN 0826-4384)
Bibliography p.
ISBN 0-88645-042-X

1. Canada - Commerce - European Economic Community.
2. European Economic Community - Commerce - Canada.
l. Institute for Research on Public Policy.
ll. Title. lll. Series.

HF1480.15.E97P36 1986   382'.0971'04   C86-090263-3

The Institute for Research on Public Policy/
L'Institut de recherches politiques
2149 Mackay Street
Montreal, Quebec H3G 2J2

Contents

List of Tables

Key to Acronyms

ACP	African, Carribean and Pacific countries
CAP	Common Agricultural Policy (of the EC)
CFDI	Canadian Foreign Direct Investment
CMEA	Council for Mutual Economic Assistance
DME	Developed Market Economies
EC	European Community
EC-10	Number of EC members referred to (e.g. EC-6 is the original six members, EC-12 is the present membership, EC-10 does not include Spain and Portugal)
ECU	European Currency Unit
EFTA	European Free Trade Association
FDI	Foreign Direct Investment
FIRA	Foreign Investment Review Agency (or Act)
GATT	General Agreement on Tariffs and Trade
GDP	Gross Domestic Product
IMF	International Monetary Fund
LDC	Less Developed Countries
MNC	Multinational Corporation

NIC	Newly Industrialized Countries
OECD	Organization for Economic Cooperation and Development
OPEC	Organization of Petroleum Exporting Countries
PEMDE	Program for Export Market Development
TNC	Transnational Corporation
U.N.	United Nations
UNCTAD	United Nations Conference on Trade and Development

Foreword

In 1976 Canada and the European Community concluded a "Framework Agreement", which was aimed at fostering closer economic relations and stimulating mutual trade and investment. Yet over the past decade flows of trade and investment between Canada and the European Community— now grown to twelve member countries—have stagnated. The entire European Community now accounts for a smaller part of Canadian exports than Japan alone.

This study by Nicolas Papadopoulos examines in detail Canada's neglected partnership with the European Community; it reviews recent developments in Canada—European Community economic relationships in the broader context of the changing patterns of their economic ties with other countries and areas; and it provides a provocative analysis of the reasons for the erosion of Canada's links across the Atlantic. The study concludes that Canada can no longer afford to neglect its partnership with the European Economic Community, the largest trading block in the world, with whose member countries we have so many strong historical, economic, cultural and political ties. Professor Papadopoulos offers a variety of challenging proposals as to ways in which Canada's economic relationship with the Community could be strengthened, without weakening Canada's important economic and trade relationship with the United States, countries of the Pacific Rim area, or other countries.

Nicolas Papadopoulos is an authority on trade and investment links between Canada and the European Community. Since 1981 he has been involved in a long-term program of research into the internationalization of Canadian business, focusing on relations with the European Community and on the perceptions of European consumers about Canadian products. This essay reflects in part that larger study. It is hoped that it will be useful to people in government and the academic community who have interests in trade policy issues, as well as to people in the private sector with interests in Canada's trade and economic relations with the European Community.

The Institute would like to thank those who gave the author their assistance and support in the course of this study, especially the School of Business at Carleton University, the Associates' Workshop in Business Research at the University of Western Ontario, the European Institute for Advanced Studies in Management in Brussels, several officials in the Department of External Affairs, and the Delegation in Ottawa of the Commission of the European Communities.

A. R. Dobell
President

September 1986

Avant-propos

En 1976, le Canada signait un accord-cadre avec la Communauté
européenne, afin de promouvoir des relations économiques plus
étroites et de stimuler les échanges commerciaux et financiers.
Pourtant, après une décennie, on constate que les échanges entre
le Canada et la Communauté européenne, qui compte
actuellement douze membres, n'ont pas évolué. Les exportations
canadiennes vers les pays de la Communauté sont inférieures à
celles vers le seul Japon.

L'étude de Nicolas Papadopoulos est consacrée à l'examen
détaillé de ce manque d'intérêt dans les relations avec la
Communauté européenne. Elle examine l'évolution récente de
cette situation, dans la perspective plus large de l'évolution
respective des échanges de chacun des deux groupes avec les
autres pays et régions. Elle fournit une analyse stimulante des
raisons de l'érosion des rapports entre le Canada et les pays
d'Outre-Atlantique.

Nicolas Papadopoulos est un expert dans le domaine des
échanges commerciaux et financiers entre le Canada et la
Communauté européenne. Depuis 1981, il poursuit ses efforts
dans le cadre d'un programme de recherche à long terme qui
porte sur l'internationalisation des activités économiques
canadiennes, se préoccupant spécialement des relations avec la
Communauté européenne et des opinions des consommateurs
européens, relativement aux produits canadiens. La présente
étude reflète partiellement cette recherche. Elle devrait s'avérer
utile pour les hommes politiques et les universitaires concernés
par les questions de commerce international, aussi bien que pour
les responsables du secteur privé canadien qui s'intéressent aux
relations économiques et commerciales avec la Communauté
européenne.

L'Institut voudrait remercier, ici, tous ceux qui ont apporté leur aide et leur soutien à l'auteur, au cours de ce travail, et notamment la School of Business de l'université Carleton, l'Associates' Workshop in Business Research de l'université du Western Ontario, l'Institut européen d'études supérieures en gestion des affaires de Bruxelles, plusieurs personnalités du Ministère des Affaires extérieures et la délégation de la Commission des Communautés européennes à Ottawa.

Acknowledgements

This essay is based on part of a project which examines issues of Canadian trade and foreign direct investment with special emphasis on the Canada-European Community relationship. Over the six years since its inception in 1981 a large number of individuals and organizations have contributed to make the project possible.

The Institute for Research on Public Policy (IRPP) sponsored the most recent phase of the research, as well as this essay. The author is particularly indebted to John M. Curtis, Director of the International Economics Program at the IRPP until 1985. Over the past few years he has given freely of his time in discussing various aspects of the study and in providing direction and support for its completion. Similarly, Frank Stone, Director of the International Economics Program since 1985, has been supportive in several ways – most importantly by offering a large number of insightful comments after an extensive review of an early draft of this manuscript.

The Associates' Workshop in Business Research of the School of Business Administration at the University of Western Ontario provided the fellowship that helped start the project in 1981. Sydney F. Wise, Dean, Faculty of Graduate Studies and Research, Dennis M. Forcese, Dean, Faculty of Social Sciences, and Antonio J. Bailetti, Director, School of Business, all at Carleton University, have provided continuous financial and other support throughout the duration of this research. The Delegation of the Commission of the European Community in Ottawa has always been helpful by making available a wealth of background materials and statistics. Finally, the European Institute for Advanced Studies in Management kindly made office space and secretarial assistance available during visits to the seat of the Community in Brussels. The help of these institutions and the support received from the individuals in them, has been indispensable to say the least.

In studies as large and as lengthy as this, the researcher needs the critical comments of dedicated colleagues who help to directly or indirectly keep the project on course. This researcher is fortunate to have many such colleagues. Grateful appreciation is especially due to Professors David Cray, George H. Haines Jr., Louise A. Heslop, and Judith J. Marshall, all at Carleton University, Gerry Hampton at Seattle University, Peter Banting at McMaster University, Françoise Graby at Université de Paris-Dauphine, Jozsef Berács at Karl Marx University in Budapest, and George Avlonitis, previously at the University of Strathclyde and now at the Athens Graduate School of Business and Economics.

A special, though certainly insufficient, note of thanks is owed to Irene Papadopoulos; having been involved in this project since the beginning, she has spent many long hours on data collection and screening, the preparation of summary reports, statistical analysis, and reviewing and commenting on several earlier drafts. In addition, many research assistants have been instrumental to the progress of this study, including Melissa Clark, Mark Leichnitz, Ann Stubbings and Catherine Frank, who collected data during various phases of the project; to their credit, they were always able to locate unpublished reports and data regardless of how carefully these were often hidden inside vast organizations and libraries.

Last, but certainly not least, a debt of gratitude is owed to the more than 150 individuals in Canada and Europe who agreed to be interviewed by, or hold discussions with, this researcher over the course of the study. Special appreciation must be expressed to Finn Olesen at the Ottawa delegation of the Community; Lauren Thibault, Frank Petrie, and Tom Burns, Presidents, respectively, of the Canadian Manufacturers' Association and of the Canadian Export Association (past and present); Harald von Riekhoff at the Department of Political Science at Carleton; J.E.G. Gibson at External Affairs; and Armand Blume, Michel Perrault, and Sydney Harris, Canada's Trade Commissioners in, respectively, Paris, Brussels, and Rome. Each of these individuals met this researcher more than once over the years, or for lengthy sessions, to provide new insights and information as the international trade scene evolved.

To all these individuals and institutions, the author expresses his sincere thanks. Naturally, any errors in this essay are his own.

The Author

Nicolas Papadopoulos is Associate Professor of Marketing and International Business at Carleton University, School of Business, Ottawa. He holds B.Com. (Athens), MBA (Washington State) and DBA (Athens) degrees. He worked in industry for five years, mainly in marketing positions, before embarking on an academic career. Dr. Papadopoulos has published over 40 articles, conference papers, monographs and books on a variety of subjects including international trade and marketing, product management, marketing theory, and marketing in times of resource shortages. His current research interests are in Canadian-European trade relationships and on the effects of country-of-origin images on consumer behavior.

In 1984, Dr. Papadopoulos helped found and became Co-ordinator of the International Business Study Group at Carleton University. The group has organized or co-sponsored several major programs, including the international symposium, "Trade Options for Canada: The Challenge for Public and Corporate Management", and a series of seminars on the views of foreign investors about the investment climate in Canada. The author is also Director of Communications and President-elect of the National Capital Chapter of the American Marketing Association, and an active member of nine professional societies in Canada, the U.S. and Europe.

Summary

The last four decades have been years of change and readjustment in the international economy. World exports and foreign direct investment grew substantially, thus increasing international interdependence. Many new and strong actors emerged on the international stage — most notably the Pacific Rim nations. The second half of this period saw the emergence of a variety of problems including slow economic growth, saturated domestic markets, stagflation, the crippling foreign debt of many less developed countries and the natural resource shortages of the 1970s, followed by record-low commodity prices in the 1980s. In the more recent period 1983-1985, there has been an uneven record of recovery and growth, characterized by lower inflation levels, fluctuating interest rates and, in several countries, persistent unemployment. Developments such as these have resulted in shifts both in the demand characteristics of markets around the world and in the comparative positions of the major trading nations.

Canada is closely linked to the international economy through both outward and inward trade and foreign direct investment. Although external trade and investment have always been seen as important to the Canadian economy, the above developments have brought about a heightened awareness of this importance to Canada's long term position in the international system.

Canada's external economic relationships have often been viewed as a zero-sum game, expressed as the so-called "continentalism vs. diversification" dilemma. This suggests a choice between Canada's major trading partner, the United States, and other markets, as alternate targets in the formulation of both public policies and business strategies. This view does not provide a framework within which present strengths can be enhanced and future trade and foreign investment opportunities can be capitalized upon. Recent initiatives, including the opening of negotiations aimed at concluding a free trade agreement with the United States, increasing Canada's presence in the Pacific Rim and attracting investors from several foreign countries, suggest that "continentalism" and "diversification" are now viewed as complementary, rather than mutually exclusive, trade options for Canada.

In this context, one potential opportunity area for improved economic partnership is the European Community (EC). Canada's trade and direct investment relationship with the EC reflects a paradox. Close historical and cultural ties, geographic proximity and a strong trade base in the early years after the Second World War, point toward the potential for high levels of economic interaction between the two partners. Yet the record shows that the importance of each partner in the other's trade has been declining steadily over the recent past. The entire European Community accounts for about six per cent of Canadian exports today, or about one-third of the level of exports to the United Kingdom alone just 25 years ago.

One explanation of the deterioration in this trade partnership was the very formation, in 1958, of the Community. By establishing an external tariff wall around the Community while abolishing most internal tariffs, the EC helped increase trade among its members and reduced their need for trade with non-member countries. Furthermore, the EC's Common Agricultural Policy (CAP) established a variety of external trade barriers and helped to improve the Community members' self-sufficiency in many agricultural sectors, which in turn resulted in a substantial reduction of Canada's agricultural exports to the area. Canada's access to one of its most important trade partners of the time, the United Kingdom, was also negatively affected when the U.K. joined the EC in 1973, since preferential access for Canadian exports to the U.K. came to an end.

While such factors have certainly played a major role in shaping today's Canada-EC relationship, they paint only an incomplete picture of what appears to be a neglected partnership. For instance, the U.K.'s share in Canadian exports had already declined from 17 per cent in 1960 to 9 per cent in 1970, three years before the U.K. became an EC member; and the formation of the EC has not had as profound an effect on the EC's other external trade partners, such as the U.S. or Japan, as it did on Canada. Several additional explanations can help to shed some light on the current low levels of economic interaction between Canada and the EC. One is the relative absence of emphasis in public policy on developing trade with the Community. Generally, attention has focused on maintaining and improving access to the U.S. market and on opening new markets for Canada in the fast-growing Pacific Rim region, rather than on West European markets which are perceived as too saturated, competitive and slow-growing to merit more attention.

Another explanation revolves around certain systemic factors which characterize the structure of the Canadian economy itself and which affect Canada's relations with both the EC and the other major industrialized countries. These include weaknesses in several manufacturing industries, the generally small size of indigenous firms, inadequacies in qualified managerial and technical personnel and the high levels of foreign ownership in Canadian industry. Considering the last of these, for example, and regardless of the merits of foreign investment insofar as the domestic economy is concerned, some sample statistics help to explain the present orientation of Canadian trade in terms of destinations. For instance, 19 of Canada's 50 largest exporting firms are foreign owned and controlled; of these, nine Japanese trading companies handle fully 71 per cent of Canada's exports to Japan.

Finally, another set of explanatory factors includes specific bilateral issues affecting the Canada-EC relationship. These include the failure of the 1976 Framework Agreement between the two entities to produce any direct and significant results; a number of irritants which have strained bilateral relations, ranging from the EC's ban of sealskin imports to Canada's import quotas on footwear; and finally, though not least in importance, the apparent unwillingness of Canadian policy and decision makers to view the EC as one entity rather than as a collection of unrelated nations.

A starting point for reviewing trade and investment between Canada and the EC can be to examine this relationship from a broader geopolitical perspective. Such a perspective would focus on the present status and potential future role of the world's major trade areas and markets. Viewing the Canada-EC relationship from this vantage point appears to suggest that further neglect of the Community as a trade partner may not be beneficial to Canada's long-term interests. As the largest trading block in the world, the European Community represents both opportunities and threats for Canada. The current low level of Community imports from Canada is in itself an opportunity. Canada's present share of EC imports is one per cent, while its share of U.S. imports is almost 20 per cent. The already high level of penetration of the U.S. market suggests a difficulty in further major gains; on the other hand, the low share of the EC import market indicates the potential for substantial improvements. Further, every additional share point of Japanese, U.S. and EC imports is worth approximately US$1.3 billion, $2.5 billion and $6 billion respectively; thus the potential net effect on Canada's exports from gains in EC markets would seem to warrant the effort necessary to achieve it.

In addition to the large size of the EC's internal market, a potential opportunity for Canadian firms can be found in the Community's extensive formal and informal trade links with a variety of nations around the world; these include the members of the European Free Trade Association (EFTA), a large number of former colonies of EC member nations, and countries in Eastern Europe. Canadian companies investing in the EC might thus gain improved access to a variety of markets beyond the Community itself. On the other hand, the same external links of the Community may be seen as potential threats to Canadian firms that do not have an operational base in Europe. The loss of a substantial part of the U.K. market, when that country joined the Community, is a primary example.

Generally, Canada is faced with increasing international competition in resource markets, mainly from less developed countries, as well as in manufacturing and advanced technology sectors, mainly from industrialized nations. Enhancing the Canada-EC relationship in the form of bilateral trade and direct investment as well as, possibly, co-operative ventures, can result in increased exports to the large EC market, improved access to several other countries and perhaps fewer competitive pressures from EC companies in international markets.

Improving Canada's position in relation to the European Community necessitates consideration of a number of Canadian trade and related policies. These would reflect a recognition of the major trade role of the Community itself, both internationally as well as in comparison to the roles played by its member nations. Such policies can include new efforts to resolve bilateral irritants; promoting Canadian "flagship" industries and products; attracting European investment in Canada; encouraging Canadian company participation in joint ventures with European firms; and more general policies aimed at enhancing the international competitiveness of Canadian manufacturing industries and at enlarging the pool of skilled managerial personnel in the Canadian economy. This essay examines the partnership between Canada and the EC in detail, and considers these and other policies that can help to change the present "uncomfortable" partnership into a more satisfying and better developed relationship for the benefit of both parties.

Abrégé

L'économie internationale a connu, au cours des quatre dernières décennies, de nombreux changements et redressements. Les exportations mondiales et les investissements directs étrangers se sont considérablement accrus, augmentant ainsi l'inter-dépendance internationale. On y a vu l'arrivée de nouveaux acteurs de poids sur la scène internationale, souvent issus de ce qu'il est convenu d'appeler la "ceinture du Pacifique". La seconde moitié de cette période a été marquée par l'apparition de différents problèmes: ralentissement de la croissance économique, saturation des marchés intérieurs, stagflation, dette extérieure écrasante en de nombreux pays en voie de développement, pénuries de ressources naturelles durant les années 1970 et baisse à un niveau record du prix des produits de base au cours des années 1980. Enfin les années 1983-1985 ont été le théâtre d'une reprise et d'une croissance économiques inégales, s'accompagnant d'une baisse de l'inflation, de la fluctuation des taux d'intérêts et, dans plusieurs pays, d'un taux de chômage obstinément élevé. Ces divers facteurs ont entraîné une modification des paramètres de la demande à travers le monde ainsi qu'un rajustement des positions comparatives des pays occupant l'avant-scène des marchés internationaux.

Par ses exportations et ses importations ainsi que par les investissements étrangers directs dont il bénéficie, le Canada est intimement lié à l'économie internationale. Si l'on connaissait déjà l'importance du commerce extérieur et des investissements étrangers pour le Canada, les transformations des dernières années ont permis d'en saisir toute l'ampleur quant à la position à long terme du Canada dans le système international.

Les relations économiques du Canada avec l'étranger ont longtemps semblé enfermées dans le dilemme opposant "continentalisme" à "diversification". Il semblait donc que le

Canada ne pouvait formuler sa politique économique et sa stratégie commerciale qu'en fonction d'un choix entre les États-Unis, son principal partenaire commercial, et les autres marchés, considérés comme solution unique de remplacement. On peut s'interroger aujourd'hui sur la justesse d'un tel point de vue et se demander s'il permet au Canada d'exploiter tous ses atouts et de profiter pleinement de toutes les possibilités qui lui sont offertes en matière de commerce extérieur et d'investissements étrangers. Un certain nombre d'interventions récentes, telles l'ouverture des négociations en vue de la conclusion éventuelle d'un accord de libre-échange avec les États-Unis ainsi que l'amorce de démarches visant à accroître la présence du Canada auprès des pays de la ceinture du Pacifique et à favoriser les investissements de plusieurs autres pays en sol canadien, attestent d'une évolution à cet égard, tendant à faire coexister continentalisme et diversification à titre d'options commerciales complémentaires.

Dans ce contexte, la Communauté économique européenne (CEE) nous offre des possibilités intéressantes de diversifier nos liens commerciaux. L'évolution des relations du Canada avec la CEE sur le plan du commerce et des investissements directs tient du paradoxe. La multiplicité des liens historiques et culturels entre les deux entités, leur proximité géographique ainsi que la base solide sur laquelle reposaient leurs relations commerciales au lendemain de la Deuxième Guerre mondiale semblent appeler un rapprochement économique étroit entre les deux partenaires. Néanmoins, l'évolution récente de leurs rapports est marquée par le déclin constant de leur importance réciproque dans leur bilan commercial extérieur. Ainsi, les divers pays de la CEE ne reçoivent plus aujourd'hui que 6 p. 100 des exportations totales du Canada, soit environ le tiers du pourcentage des exportations canadiennes à destination du Royaume-Uni seulement il y a 25 ans.

Cette détérioration est attribuable en partie à la création, en 1958, de la CEE. En érigeant une barrière douanière autour des pays qui la composent et en supprimant la plupart des droits de douane internes, la CEE a stimulé les échanges commerciaux entre pays membres, réduisant leur besoin de commercer avec les non-membres. En outre, la politique agricole commune (PAC) de la CEE est venue imposer une série d'obstacles tarifaires au commerce avec les pays non membres et a favorisé l'auto-suffisance des pays membres, ce qui a forcé le Canada à réduire de façon considérable ses exportations agricoles à destination de l'Europe. Les échanges du Canada avec le Royaume-Uni, l'un de ses principaux partenaires commerciaux à l'époque ont par ailleurs subi le contrecoup de l'entrée de ce dernier dans la CEE en 1973, en raison de la suppression du tarif spécial dont ils avaient jusqu'alors bénéficié.

Ces divers facteurs ont certes contribué à façonner les relations actuelles entre le Canada et la CEE, mais ils ne peuvent rendre totalement compte d'une situation, qui découle en partie de la négligence. La part des exportations canadiennes vers le Royaume-Uni avait ainsi déjà chuté de 17 p. 100 en 1960 à 9 p. 100 en 1970, trois ans avant que ce dernier ne se joigne au Marché Commun. Par ailleurs, les relations commerciales entretenues avec leurs partenaires européens par des pays comme les États-Unis et le Japon n'ont pas autant souffert de la création de la CEE. Plusieurs autres facteurs peuvent donc expliquer la faiblesse des échanges commerciaux entre le Canada et la CEE. À titre d'exemple, on peut souligner le manque de vigueur dont a fait preuve le Canada pour accroître ses échanges avec l'Europe. En effet, le Canada s'est surtout efforcé de maintenir et d'améliorer la pénétration de ses produits sur le marché américain et d'ouvrir de nouveaux marchés dans les pays à croissance rapide de la ceinture du Pacifique, délaissant ainsi les pays de l'Europe de l'Ouest, dont les marchés étaient jugés saturés, relativement figés et trop compétitifs.

Certaines caractéristiques propres à la structure de l'économie canadienne viennent également expliquer la nature des rapports commerciaux entretenus par le Canada tant avec la CEE qu'avec les principaux pays industrialisés. Il s'agit entre autres de la faiblesse de plusieurs industries manufacturières, de la taille relativement modeste des entreprises proprement canadiennes, de l'insuffisance de gestionnaires et de techniciens compétents ainsi que de l'importance de la mainmise étrangère dans le secteur industriel. À cet égard, et quels que soient les avantages que tire le Canada des investissements étrangers sur son territoire, l'analyse des statistiques commerciales permet de mieux comprendre l'orientation actuelle des échanges du Canada en ce qui a trait à la destination de ses exportations. Ainsi, 19 des 50 principales sociétés commerciales du Canada au chapitre des exporations appartiennent à des intérêts étrangers; de ce nombre, on compte neuf entreprises japonaises, assurant 71 p. 100 du volume des exportations à destination du Japon.

Enfin, d'autres explications ont trait à un certain nombre de questions découlant précisément des rapports Canada-CEE, tels l'incapacité de l'Entente cadre conclue en 1976 entre les deux parties de générer des résultats tangibles importants, l'existence d'un certain nombre d'"irritants", source de tension entre les partenaires (allant de l'interdiction décrétée par la CEE sur l'imporation des peaux de bébés phoques au contingentement par le Canada de ses importations de chaussures), et, facteur d'importance, le manque d'empressement manifesté par les décideurs et gouvernants canadiens à voir dans la CEE une véritable entité plutôt qu'un simple regroupement de pays disparates.

On peut par ailleurs procéder à l'étude des échanges commerciaux et des investissements entre le Canada et la CEE en adoptant une perspective géopolitique élargie, de façon à déterminer la position actuelle et le rôle futur des principaux marchés commerciaux dans le monde. Pareille démarche révèle que la non-reconnaissance de la CEE comme partenaire commercial desservirait les intérêts à long terme du Canada. À titre de premier bloc commercial au monde, la CEE présente pour le Canada à la fois des possibilités et des risques. La faiblesse actuelle des importations de la CEE de produits canadiens est elle-même porteuse d'espoirs. La part du Canada dans les importations de la CEE n'atteint que 1 p. 100, alors qu'elle est de 20 p. 100 aux États-Unis. Si la pénétration déjà importante du marché américain laisse supposer des difficultés d'amélioration à ce chapitre, le faible volume des exportations canadiennes sur les marchés européens permet d'espérer des progrès considérables. En outre, chaque point supplémentaire gagné par les importations canadiennes sur les marchés japonais, américain et européen y vaut respectivement environ 1,3 million, 2,5 millions et 6 millions de dollars (US); les conséquences pour les exportations canadiennes de tout gain obtenu sur les marchés européens semblent donc justifier l'effort nécessaire à leur réalisation.

En plus de pénétrer le marché imposant de la CEE, les entreprises canadiennes qui verraient leurs efforts couronnés de succès, pourraient tirer avantage du vaste réseau de relations, officielles et officieuses, qu'entretiennent ses membres avec un grand nombre de pays à travers le monde, qu'il s'agisse des membres de l'Association européenne de libre-échange, des anciennes colonies européennes ou encore des pays de l'Est. L'investissement dans les pays membres de la CEE peut ainsi ouvrir les portes de divers marchés extérieurs à cette dernière. Par contre, la nature des liens entretenus par la CEE avec ces divers pays peut évidemment présenter certains risques pour les entreprises canadiennes qui sont dépourvues d'une base d'exploitation en Europe. La perte d'une part importante du marché britannique lors de l'entrée du Royaume-Uni dans la CEE est, à cet égard, éloquente.

De façon générale, le Canada doit faire face à une concurrence de plus en plus vive sur les marchés internationaux, exercée, dans le secteur des ressources naturelles, par les pays en voie de développement et, dans les secteurs de la fabrication et des technologies de pointe, par les pays industrialisés. L'amélioration des relations commerciales entre le Canada et la CEE par la voie d'échanges bilatéraux, d'investissements directs ou peut-être même de projets conjoints, pourrait se traduire par l'augmentation des exportations sur le marché européen, un meilleur accès à d'autres marchés et, éventuellement, un allègement de la concurrence exercée par les entreprises européennes sur les marchés internationaux.

L'amélioration de la position du Canada auprès de la CEE exige la révision de la politique commerciale canadienne actuelle; on pourrait ainsi adopter un certain nombre de mesures visant, entre autres, à supprimer réellement les irritants mutuels, à promouvoir les industries et les produits canadiens les plus prometteurs, à stimuler les investissements européens en sol canadien, à inciter les entreprises canadiennes à former des coentreprises avec les sociétés européennes et, de façon plus générale à accroître la compétitivité internationale du secteur manufacturier canadien et à élargir le bassin des compétences en gestion dont dispose l'économie canadienne. La présente étude scrute les relations commerciales entre le Canada et la CEE, et analyse les mesures que le Canada pourrait adopter pour éliminer le caractère actuellement "inconfortable" de ces relations et les transformer en rapports plus satisfaisants et plus étoffés, qui profiteraient également aux deux parties.

Introduction

Canada is one of the 10 largest industrialized market economies in the world. It is a member of the "Summit Group of Seven" and an important actor in global political and economic affairs. It accounts for about 20 per cent of the imports of the largest single importer in the world, the United States; for approximately 4 per cent of outward and 18 per cent of inward foreign direct investment by and in developed market economies; and for about 4 per cent of world exports. On aggregate, Canada's exports represent 23 per cent of its Gross Domestic Product (GDP).

On the other side of the Atlantic, the European Community (or "Communities", as it is often referred to), can be considered as the largest experiment in economic and political integration in recent history. Following three membership enlargements[1] it now consists of 12 member nations — Belgium, Denmark, the Federal Republic of Germany, France, Greece, Ireland, Italy, Luxembourg, the Netherlands, Portugal, Spain and the United Kingdom — and is run by five major institutions. Although the extent of the success (or failure) of this experiment is open to debate, especially in the political sphere, it has nonetheless resulted in the creation of the largest trading block in the world.

Collectively, the present members have a population of 320 million; they account for about 35 per cent of world exports and imports; for about 50 per cent of each other's trade; and for approximately 33 per cent of outward and 46 per cent of inward foreign direct investment (FDI) by or in developed market economies (DMEs). Similarly to Canada, European Community (EC) exports account for about 25 per cent of its Gross Domestic Product.

At first glance, one might reasonably expect to find a strong trading partnership between Canada and the EC. Both depend heavily on exports. Both are developed market economies, yet a

1

certain complementarity exists between them, given Canada's strength and the EC's weakness in resources. Finally, the two traditional preconditions for effective trade development are also present in this bilateral relationship: geographic proximity and cultural affinity. These are especially relevant in the case of the U.K., with which Canada, as a member of the British Commonwealth, has had traditional close ties, as well as in the cases of both the U.K. and France, with which Canada's English and French subcultures have had strong historic and cultural links.

Yet in spite of these and other positive factors, the trade relationship between the two partners is undeveloped and occasionally uncomfortable, and appears to be deteriorating. This is true both generally, concerning Canada's economic relations with the EC overall, and specifically in regards to Canadian-U.K. trade. As recently as 1960, 17 per cent of all Canadian exports went to the United Kingdom alone[2]. By 1970, just before the U.K. joined the Community, this proportion had dropped to 9 per cent. Canadian exports to the EC as a whole[3], including the U.K., stood at 16 per cent in the same year. By 1980 the U.K. accounted for 4 per cent, and the entire Community (again including the U.K.) for 13 per cent, of total Canadian exports. Finally, by 1984, these proportions had dropped to 2 per cent and 6 per cent respectively. Thus the EC's relative importance in Canadian exports is about one-third of what the U.K.'s importance alone was just 25 years ago.

Similarly with imports: the U.K. by itself accounted for 11 per cent of the Canadian total in 1960, but for only 5 per cent in 1970, 3 per cent in 1980, and 2.4 per cent in 1984. The total EC share in Canadian imports, including the U.K., dropped somewhat more slowly from 11 per cent to 8 per cent between 1970 and 1980; by 1984 it had stabilized at about 8.5 per cent.

At the general level, there are at least six possible explanations for this decline in importance of the EC to Canada, and vice versa, as trade partners: first, the increasing concentration of Canada's trade in the U.S. since the end of the Second World War, at which time the shattered West European economies declined in relative importance for Canada; second, the creation of the EC itself, which erected a common external tariff wall in 1958 and then embraced Canada's traditional trade partner, the U.K., in 1973; third, the slow growth of the European economies since the early 1970s, which made them less attractive to Canadian exporters; fourth, the small size of the Canadian economy which, in and of itself, is of relatively little importance to EC firms; fifth, the appreciation of the Canadian dollar against

European currencies during the early 1980s which made Canadian goods more expensive in Europe; sixth, the relative rise in importance of countries in the Pacific Rim as trade destinations, which has been attracting the interest of Canadian and European exporters alike since the late 1970s.

While such factors are valid, however, they are not enough to explain the lack of vigour and steep decline in Canada-EC trade. After all, none of these is unique to Canada. Further, unlike other non-EC countries such as Japan or the U.S., Canada has a "framework agreement" designed to encourage trade with the Community; its currency is not as strong as that of the U.S. against European currencies; and it has not experienced the kind of undeclared trade war that Japan has faced in Europe in the past four to five years. Canada is also significantly larger or has a much stronger economy than several other non-EC countries such as Brazil, Sweden, Australia, or Finland. Yet, none of the sample countries mentioned here, from the U.S. to Finland, has experienced the problems and difficulties exemplified by the rapid decline in trade between the Community and Canada.

What, then, are the unique factors that affect Canadian-EC trade? What can explain the paradox of declining trade between two entities which would normally be expected to be close partners? Further, should this decline be cause for concern among the Canadian policy-makers? If so, what policies might be worthy of consideration in order to reverse this trend? These are the main questions that are addressed in this essay.

Stated differently, this study has a three-fold objective: to analyse recent trends in trade and investment flows between Canada and the European Community and the reasons behind them; to examine the potential impact of further disengagement in the Canadian-EC trade and direct investment relationship upon Canada's competitive[4] position in the international arena; and to discuss policy alternatives which could be considered by Canada in its efforts to strengthen its international trade presence, especially in relation to its competitive position in and against the European Community.

This study assumes a policy perspective from the Canadian viewpoint. The issue is the need to identify the appropriate policy questions that Canada must consider in relation to trade and investment with the EC. Nonetheless, some policy issues from the European side are also addressed where necessary.

Discussion in this essay focuses on general, economy-wide considerations. Individual issues pertaining to provinces of Canada, member states of the EC, or economic sectors on either side of the Atlantic are examined only where necessary and relevant to the objectives. This by no means implies that the relative importance of various sectors of Canada or individual provinces, to the EC or its individual members, is generally the same. Trade in agriculture and resources is more vital to Canada's western provinces, while trade in manufactures is more important to central Canada; further, Canada's bilateral trade and investment relationship is more important in relation to the U.K. or France than in relation to Greece or Luxembourg. To discuss such relationships in more detail, however, would present two problems: first, to do so, while still doing justice to the subjects involved, would require a separate, extensive study for each province-sector-country combination; second, it would negate the advantages of a more general perspective which reflects the combined effect of actions and events, past or future, that have shaped or will shape the Canada-EC relationship.

Three types of sources were used in this research: interviews and discussions with experts on Canadian, EC, or Canadian-EC trade and investment; published statistical information; and research, analyses and perspectives in the literature on the same topics. In addition to the usual limitations of the first two of these sources[5], there is a relative paucity of research in Canada concerning trade and investment specifically with the Community. Besides a handful of studies dealing with specific economic issues (e.g. Nadeau, 1985, on agricultural trade with the U.K.; Abdel-Malek, 1983, on Canadian FDI in the Community), the only other references are found in more general research such as, for example, on the export destinations preferred by Canadian producers (where the EC is just one of several destinations mentioned). In light of this, a useful by-product of the present study has been the compilation of a near-exhaustive Canadian bibliography on its subject matter. This bibliography is supplemented with relevant studies from the literature in the U.S. and Europe.

The essay is divided into four chapters. The first two provide an overview of Canada and the EC respectively as actors on the international economic stage. The intent here is *not* to provide separate and detailed descriptions of either partner's trade performance independently of the other, since this has been the subject of numerous other studies. Rather, these first chapters aim to highlight those factors in each entity's international performance that have a bearing on its relationship with the other. Against the background of Chapters I and II, Chapter III examines specifically the evolution and present status of trade and direct investment between the EC and Canada, and traces the factors that have led to the present state of affairs. Finally, Chapter IV considers the potential impact of the relationship for Canada and the issues involved in developing successful policies for a smoother and better developed partnership with the EC.

Notes

1. The original signatories of the Treaty of Rome, which established the Community in 1958, were Belgium, Luxembourg, France, the Netherlands, Italy and the Federal Republic of Germany. The United Kingdom, Ireland, and Denmark joined in the first enlargement of 1973. The second enlargement occurred in 1981 when Greece became the tenth member. Spain and Portugal joined on January 1, 1986.

2. All statistical data that appear in the Introduction are taken from the tables in the four chapters that follow.

3. Because of their very recent entry into the Community, trade and investment statistics for Spain and Portugal have not yet been integrated with those of the EC. Therefore, references to the Community from this point on include the statistics of its first 10 members only. Given the small size of these economies in relation to the "Community of Ten", this does not materially affect the discussion in this essay. Specific reference to these countries is made, however, whenever their membership is likely to have an effect on the Canada-EC relationship (e.g. fisheries and agriculture). Timely discussions on the ramifications of the EC's third enlargement are, at this point, limited to the general press. An interesting overview of these ramifications, especially concerning Spain, may be found in the Financial Times (see References, "Spain and the EEC 1986").

4. The term "competitive" is used throughout the essay in the strategic, managerial sense. A nation's international competitiveness reflects the aggregate attributes (e.g. quality, design, price, distribution, market share) of its products and industries in foreign markets, in relation to those from other markets. Thus competitiveness determines not only a nation's present performance in world trade but also the ease or difficulty with which it can penetrate existing markets or open new ones.

5.   *Sources*: About 50 personal interviews with government, business, and academic experts were conducted at the beginning of the project in 1981-1982. Discussions and interviews with approximately 100 more individuals in similar positions were held between 1982 and late 1985. A small number of additional discussions were held between March and December 1985 with some of the key respondents from the earlier series, in order to bring previously expressed views up to date.

An adapted form of the "key informant" technique (a non-probability sampling method; see Houston and Sudman 1975, Phillips 1980) was used in identifying interviewees. Individuals in appropriate key positions, whose nature implies knowledgeability on the subject being researched, were interviewed and then asked to name additional experts as potential interviewees. Each successive group of respondents provided additional suggestions, until a satisfactory cross-section of experts had been interviewed. This process lends itself to this type of research in view of the difficulty of identifying appropriate interview subjects. All individuals approached for this study occupied high-ranking positions within their respective organizations (e.g. presidents of trade associations; bureau chiefs at Canadian government departments and directors-general of the appropriate directorates at the EC's Commission in Brussels; and corporate presidents or vice-presidents of Canadian or foreign firms).

Fifty-nine per cent of the total were Canadians, 39 per cent were Europeans, and 2 per cent were Americans. Twenty-five per cent occupied positions in Canadian federal and provincial governments; 16 per cent were EC and member-government officials; 38 per cent were business executives of Canadian, European, and U.S. firms; 17 per cent occupied academic positions in Canada and Europe; finally, 4 per cent represented trade and related associations.

Concerning other background sources, the paucity of publications both in Canada and in Europe, addressing specifically Canada-EC trade issues, is noted above. In terms of statistical data, the latest available figures are used; this does not imply uniformity in the data cited because of the time delay involved and the variety of methods used in reports by the major international agencies.

For Canada, trade figures for 1984 are available from Statistics Canada; these are used wherever independent Canadian figures are cited. The latest available statistics for world-wide trade are those of the International Monetary Fund (IMF) for 1983 in "Directions of Trade" and, for some sectoral details, those of the Organization for Economic Co-operation and Development (OECD) for 1982. Whenever comparisons between Canada and other countries are necessary, therefore, the 1983 or 1982 figures are used. For detailed statistics on EC trade, the main source is EUROSTAT, the Community's statistical agency; the latest data are for 1983 and, in some cases, 1982. The same is true for data on the European Free Trade Association (EFTA). Statistics on foreign direct investment are much older and, with few exceptions, reach only up to 1979 (OECD and United Nations Centre on Transnational Corporations).

The detailed Canadian figures are reported by Statistics Canada in Canadian dollars; the IMF, OECD, and EFTA use U.S. dollars; EUROSTAT reports in ECUs (European Currency Units). In view of currency fluctuations and the variety of methods used in establishing conversion rates by the reporting organizations, there is a wide gulf between the statistics reported by them. For instance, IMF shows a decline in world exports between 1980 and 1983, while EUROSTAT shows an increase for the same period. This report uses the most relevant source in each case, always in the original currency cited. Differences between the figures reported by various organizations are noted where necessary. Also noted are deviations from normal statistical valuation methods in agency reports. Normally, all exports are given in f.o.b. prices, all imports are c.i.f., and all "export" figures include both domestic exports and re-exports.

Chapter I:

Canada's Comparative Trade and Investment Position

International Markets or Die.
R.C. Scrivener
President, Northern Telecom
1979

1. World Trends

Business activity has become international in scope. By the early 1980s world exports had increased to about US$2.0 trillion, up seven times from about US$300 billion in 1970. Similar increases have been recorded in foreign direct investment (FDI). The stock of FDI by developed market economies (DMEs) rose three-fold from US$112 billion to $372 billion between 1967 and 1978. While the rapid growth of trade in the 1960s and 1970s slowed down and was, in fact, negative between 1981 and 1983[1], past trends have already resulted in what is often referred to in terms such as the "globalization of markets", "the world economy", or "the era of interdependence" (see, for example, Levitt 1983).

The internationalization of business activity can be attributed to four inter-related sets of factors. Most of these have special significance for Canada. The first consists of those general environmental variables that facilitate the international movement of goods, capital, people, and information (e.g. communications, transportation, relative international stability). The second reflects the rationale which lies behind the need of individual firms to internationalize. Of the many factors that comprise this rationale[2], four have had, and will continue to have, a growing importance for Canadian business: the need to escape from slow-growing domestic markets (whether because of recessionary, demographic, competitive, or other pressures); the need to maintain a technological edge; the need to avoid the diseconomies of small-scale production; and the need for market power and prestige.

The third set arises from the emergence of new and significant actors on the international economic scene. Until the late 1960s, international business activity was most often

9

identified with the strong presence of U.S. goods and FDI world-wide. Today, the U.S. is deeply concerned about a large, and rapidly growing, trade deficit. Its share of world exports declined from 16 per cent in 1960 to 12 per cent in 1983, while that of Japan rose from 3 per cent to 9 per cent in the same period and that of the non-OPEC Less Developed Countries (LDC) rose from 16 per cent to 19 per cent between 1977 and 1983. Similarly, the stock of FDI by the U.S. declined, as a percentage of the DME total, from 50 per cent to 45 per cent between 1967-1978; in the same period, Japan's share rose from 1 per cent to 7 per cent, West Germany's from 3 per cent to 9 per cent, and Switzerland's from 3 per cent to 8 per cent.

The fourth and last set of factors that accounts for the rapid increase in international economic activity results from the combined pressure that arises from the preceding three: as individual firms attempt to expand, and as new competitors acquire or pursue strong market positions, most governments in DMEs are being forced into taking a more pro-active stance in regard to international business. In LDCs, government support for export development has been the cornerstone of industrialization for at least two decades[3]. Until recently, however, businesses in industrialized markets were largely left to fend for themselves in the international arena. What sparked the change in attitude on the part of both business and governments in many DMEs, especially in the post-1980 period, was the realization that not only their exports, but also their domestic markets, were being threatened by the emergent countries in world trade and capital flows.

For example, U.S. imports from Japan rose two-and-a-half times between 1976 and 1982, accompanied by an increase in Japan's share from 13 per cent to 16 per cent. Similarly, the flow of FDI into the U.S. from all sources increased six-fold between 1970 and 1979 (from US$1.5 billion to US$9.7 billion) while the corresponding increase of FDI flows into Canada and Western Europe was only two-fold during the same period (U.N. Centre on TNCs 1983). Along the same lines, the stock of British FDI in the U.S. doubled in the period 1981-1984 alone (from US$19 billion to US$38 billion; International Business Perspectives 1986).

What the preceding discussion points to is, in effect, a trend toward a fundamental restructuring in international trade and investment flows. This shift was identified as early as 1978. In an article aptly titled "Multinationals: the End of U.S. Dominance", Franco (1978:95-96) showed that the number of American firms among the largest 156 companies in 13 principal industry sectors world-wide declined from 111 to 68 between

1959 and 1976. At the same time, the number of West European firms within this group increased from 39 to 65 and that of Japanese firms from one to 20.

These shifts, along with the overall internationalization of the world economy, have not been reflected in the Canada-EC relationship; this is of particular interest to this essay and will be discussed in more detail below. At this point it should be noted that the complexity and implications of this restructuring has led some researchers (e.g. Kirpalani 1985) to suggest the adoption of a geopolitical perspective on world trade; this is felt to be the best means for understanding, and coping with, the new conditions in the international economic environment.

The geopolitical perspective suggests that, following the maturation of Western Europe and Japan, new competition is likely to come first from the "Third Wave Multinationals" which originate in Newly Industrialized Countries (NIC) and, possibly not long thereafter, from the increasing international activity on the part of Eastern Socialist economies (see, for example, Ting 1980; Forbes 1980; Kotler, Fahey and Jatusripitak 1985; Papadopoulos and Berács 1985).

This perspective has been adopted for the purposes of this study and will be discussed in more detail later. For now, the relevant question is: How well is Canada positioned in relation to its international competitors?

2. Canada's International Economic Performance

Tables I and II compare Canada to various other regions and countries in terms of exports and FDI respectively. They show, at the very least, a satisfactory performance. Canada ranks 8th in FDI and is one of a handful of countries that managed to actually increase their exports in 1983[4]. Further, Canada has maintained a relatively high exports-to-GDP ratio (23 per cent in 1984; see below and Table IX), and is the only OECD country besides West Germany to achieve a positive trade balance every year since 1976 (EUROSTAT 1984). On aggregate, the OECD group's deficit was US$66 billion in 1982 and US$58 billion in 1983, compared to Canadian surpluses of US$14 billion and US$12 billion in the same years (OECD Main Economic Indicators 1985).

Thus, in view of its relatively small domestic economy and population size, its brief history as a nation, and its relatively recent entry in the foreign trade and investment arena, Canada's

TABLE I. Trends in World Exports 1977-1983

1. Value of Exports in million U.S.$ (current)

Year	Developed Market Economies					All Other Countries				World[4]
	Canada	U.S.	E C[1]	Japan	DME Total[2]	Developing Oil-exporters	Developing Others	Eastern[3] Socialist	"All Other" Total	
1977	43,554	121,306	382,677	81,084	716,100	147,258	168,441	33,400	349,099	1,041,100
1979	58,298	182,007	577,513	102,293	1,052,800	208,853	248,483	49,635	506,971	1,526,200
1980	67,730	220,781	665,896	130,435	1,239,500	299,538	316,384	58,769	674,691	1,875,100
1981	72,726	233,739	612,511	151,500	1,218,500	277,748	326,641	55,683	660,072	1,845,300
1982	70,454	212,274	590,003	138,443	1,154,700	222,294	312,861	56,154	591,309	1,712,400
1983	76,745	200,535	574,496	147,000	1,139,900	192,700	323,626	53,483	569,809	1,671,200

2. Export Growth, 1977=100

Year	Canada	U.S.	E C[1]	Japan	DME Total[2]	Developing Oil-exporters	Developing Others	Eastern[3] Socialist	"All Other" Total	World[4]
1977	100	100	100	100	100	100	100	100	100	100
1979	134	150	151	126	147	142	148	149	145	147
1980	156	182	174	161	173	203	188	176	193	180
1981	167	193	160	187	170	189	194	167	189	177
1982	162	175	154	171	161	151	186	168	169	164
1983	176	165	150	181	159	131	192	160	163	161

3. Shares in World Exports (%)

Year	Canada	U.S.	E C[1]	Japan	DME Total[2]	Developing Oil-exporters	Developing Others	Eastern[3] Socialist	"All Other" Total	World[4]
1977	4.2	11.7	36.8	7.8	68.8	14.1	16.2	3.2	33.5	100
1979	3.8	11.9	37.8	6.7	69.0	13.7	16.3	3.3	32.2	100
1980	3.6	11.8	35.5	7.0	66.1	16.0	16.9	3.1	36.0	100
1981	3.9	12.7	33.2	8.2	66.0	15.1	17.7	3.0	35.8	100
1982	4.1	12.4	34.5	8.1	67.4	13.0	18.3	3.3	34.5	100
1983	4.6	12.0	34.4	8.8	68.2	11.5	19.4	3.2	34.1	100

Notes: (1) Includes intra-EC trade.
        (2) Includes Australia, New Zealand, and non-EC countries in Western Europe.
        (3) Estimates based on IMF data.
        (4) World totals are those provided by IMF; since the figures for Eastern Socialist countries are estimates, this total does not equal the arithmetic sum of the preceding columns.

Source: EUROSTAT Monthly External Trade Bulletin 1958-1983; Special Number, July 1984. Also IMF Direction of Trade Statistics, Yearbook 1984.

TABLE II. Developed Market Economies: Flows and Stock of Foreign Direct Investment
(percentage distribution)

	1. FDI Flows						2. Cumulative FDI Stock					
	Outward Flows (avg./year)			Inward Flows (avg./year)			Outward Stock			Inward Stock		
Country	1961-1967	1968-1973	1974-1978	1961-1967	1968-1973	1974-1978	1967	1973	1978	1967	1973	1978
Canada	1.6	2.8	3.7	13.5	10.0	3.0	3.3	3.8	3.7	26.6	23.4	17.7
U.S.	66.8	58.3	48.1	10.7	16.7	30.7	50.4	48.9	45.2	13.7	14.7	16.7
Japan	1.6	4.0	7.5	1.6	1.4	0.9	1.3	5.0	7.2	0.8	0.8	0.9
Australia	0.5	0.9	0.8	12.8	10.7	7.4	0.4	0.2	0.3	7.5	5.2	4.4
Belgium & Lux.	0.5[1]	0.9	1.4	3.8[1]	5.1	7.6	1.1	1.1	1.3	1.9	2.7	3.9
France	4.9	3.2	4.6	6.8	6.9	10.5	5.3	4.3	4.0	4.2	4.1	6.1
W. Germany	4.9	7.6	9.6	17.6	13.7	11.8	2.6	5.8	8.5	5.0	9.3	12.0
Italy	2.4	2.1	1.1	9.5	6.9	4.2	1.9	1.5	0.9	3.6	4.8	4.2
Netherlands	3.0	4.2	5.6	3.9	7.2	4.3	9.8	7.4	6.4	6.8	5.4	5.3
Sweden	1.3	1.5	2.0	2.0	1.4	0.3	1.5	1.4	1.6	0.7	0.7	0.5
Switzerland	NA	NA	NA	NA	NA	NA	3.3	4.9	7.5	0.5	1.6	3.2
U.K.	12.3	13.2	13.7	14.4	13.2	11.9	15.6	13.0	11.0	11.4	12.4	13.3
South Africa	NA	NA	NA	NA	NA	NA	1.7	1.0	1.0	10.0	5.7	4.4
Other DMEs (W. Europe, New Zealand)	0.2	1.3	1.9	3.4	6.8	7.4	1.8	1.7	1.4	7.3	9.2	7.4
Total:	100.0	100.0	100.0	100.0	100.0	100.0	100.0	100.0	100.0	100.0	100.0	100.0

Notes: (1) From 1965
Source: United Nations Centre on Transnational Corporations, "Salient Features and Trends in Foreign Direct Investment"; New York 1983.

performance in the international economy appears to be excellent. Stated differently, there is no question that Canada's strength in foreign markets often is inversely proportional to its small size, and that it is one of the major performers among the world's large trading nations.

Yet this optimistic appraisal is diluted when one considers several problems that permeate its foreign trade and investment activity. The need to improve upon the weaknesses so as to maintain and build upon the strengths will be a recurring theme throughout this essay. Since it examines a deteriorating relationship between Canada and one of its major partners, the following discussion often focuses more on weaknesses than on strengths. This is made necessary, as well, because of the future-oriented, geopolitical perspective that was mentioned above; for, while there is no doubt about Canada's present strength, there is also no question that several measures must be undertaken if this is to be maintained, and hopefully improved, in the future.

Some of the problems that were alluded to above include Canada's small domestic economy, the concentration of its international activity in the U.S.[5], the comparative weakness of its manufacturing sector, relatively high costs of production and rates of "labour days lost" because of industrial disputes, and the occasionally slow adoption of the new technologies (e.g., robotics; Bocker and Toon 1984). These weaknesses have been studied extensively in the literature, and do not need to be discussed in detail here. Rather, the following few pages summarize the key points that are relevant to the analysis of Canadian-European Community trade that follows, as well as the main reasons that lie behind them.

2.1. *Exports and FDI Development*
As mentioned, Canada's export-to-GDP ratio is relatively high. This statement leads to the obvious question: relative to what? The following data show that the contribution of exports to domestic production is higher in Canada than in the U.S., Japan, France, Italy, and the U.K. However, it is the same as or significantly lower than that of the other countries – most notably Norway, the Netherlands, and Belgium-Luxembourg, but also West Germany and Sweden.

Ratio of Exports-to-GDP

Country	1976	1980	1983	Country	1976	1980	1983
U.S.	6.8	7.6	7.0	West Germany	22.9	22.5	27.7
Japan	12.1	10.3	13.0	Sweden	24.8	25.9	27.0
France	16.1	17.2	17.1	Denmark	23.7	21.8	27.5
Italy	21.5	22.3	21.1	Switzerland	26.3	27.9	26.9
U.K.	21.1	22.6	21.1	Norway	25.3	29.1	31.2
				Netherlands	45.0	42.8	48.1
Canada	**19.8**	**24.6**	**23.0**	Belgium + Lux.	48.0	49.3	62.2

(Source: EUROSTAT Basic Statistics of the Community, annual)

It can be argued that Canada's export profile should be closer to the second than to the first group of countries because of the relative size of the economies involved. For example, in terms of GDP Canada is much more similar to the Netherlands and Belgium (twice and three times as large, respectively) than to Japan and the U.S. (one-fourth and one-tenth as small). Thus, while its export performance is strong in relation to the major economies of the world, it is not nearly as strong when compared with countries that share a similar need for exports.

This may partially be the result of Canada's slower rate of export growth than almost all other regions up to 1982, which in turn resulted in a steadily declining share of world exports in the years up to 1980 (Table I). Although the decline was arrested and reversed starting in 1981, it is still too early to tell whether this reflects a long-term strengthening of Canadian exports. This reversal may have been partially a delayed (and theoretically expected) result of the Canadian dollar devaluation between 1976 and 1978. However, more recent developments do not necessarily support this hypothesis. In spite of the continuing weakness of the Canadian dollar, exports rose more slowly than imports (7.4 per cent vs. 11.3 per cent) in the first three quarters of 1985 over the same period for 1984, thus reducing the cumulative merchandise trade surplus by about $2 billion and stabilizing Canada's share of world exports at about 4.5 per cent (International Business Perspectives 1986).

Alternatively, Canada's relative standing today may partially be the result of the re-adjustment of world export shares due to the steep *decline in the share* of the petroleum exporting countries (from 16 per cent to 11.5 per cent between 1980 and

1983), following the oil glut; this has similarly benefited the *share* performance not only of Canada but also of all DMEs.

Canada's foreign investment position has many similarities with that of its exports. As Table II shows, average annual outward CFDI flows increased from 1.6 per cent to 3.7 per cent of the DME total from1961 to 1967 and from 1974 to 1978. This growth represents an increase in value from an average of US$144 million to US$1.1 billion per year, which enabled Canada to maintain its share of FDI stock at about 3.7 per cent. This performance is better than that of the two traditional investor countries, the U.S. and the U.K., but significantly worse than that of newer investors such as Japan, West Germany and Switzerland, whose shares of FDI stock rose from two to six times during the same period.

2.2. *Destinations of Canadian Exports and CFDI*

In and of themselves, the lower proportions of Canadian exports and FDI over recent years may not be causes for concern. They become so because of the strong trade relationship between this country and the U.S. The two countries are each other's largest trade and investment partners. The U.S. accounts for about 75 per cent of Canadian trade, while Canada represents about 20 per cent of the United States' exports and imports. Table III shows recent trends in Canada's trade interdependence with U.S. As can be seen, the weakness of the Canadian dollar in relation to its American counterpart has helped drive even higher the already high concentration in Canada's export destinations.

Further, Table IV compares the regional distribution of Canada's exports to that of the EC, the U.S. and Japan. The wider diversification of the other major DMEs becomes immediately apparent from this table. Even within the EC, whose smaller members have access to the Community's vast "internal" market, the trade concentration ratios are considerably lower than Canada's . For example, the highest intra-EC concentration ratio is that of the Netherlands, at 72 per cent (see Table IX). This, however, represents Dutch exports to the other nine EC members combined. On a country-by-country basis, the highest concentrations are found in the U.K.'s and West Germany's share of exports by Ireland and the Netherlands, respectively (58 per cent and 40 per cent). More generally, no other country in the world is as dependent on another for its external trade as Canada is on the U.S.

Whether this trade relationship is beneficial to Canada, and whether or not the two countries should move toward a

TABLE III. Canadian Exports to and Imports from the U.S.

Year	Exports to the U.S. as a percentage of total Canadian exports	Imports from the U.S. as a percentage of total Canadian imports
1980	63	70
1981	66	69
1982	68	71
1983	73	72
1984	76	72

Sources: Statistics Canada Exports-Merchandise Trade (annual, Cat.65-202)
Statistics Canada Imports-Merchandise Trade (annual, Cat.65-203)

TABLE IV. Export Destinations

Exporting Country	Export Destinations (1983)					
	EC-10	U.S.	Japan	Canada	Rest of World	Total Exports
EC-10	51.5[1]	6.7	1.1	0.7	40.0	100
U.S.	22.5	-	9.9	18.0	49.6	100
Japan	12.9	27.6	-	2.6	56.9	100
Canada	6.4	76.0	5.0	-	12.6	100

Note: (1) This percentage is intra-Community trade; if this is excluded, of course, EC's trade diversification is even broader.

Sources: EUROSTAT Monthly External Trade Bulletin 1958-1983; Special Number, July 1984.
Statistics Canada Exports-Merchandise Trade (annual, Cat.65-202)

comprehensive or sectoral trade agreement between them (in which direction the governments of both countries are now moving) are issues that lie beyond the scope of this discussion. What is relevant here is that, in view of the heavy concentration of Canadian trade to and from the U.S., Canada's share of world exports greatly overstates its actual presence in markets outside of North America.

Of Canada's $112 billion in 1984 exports, only 24 per cent ($27 billion) reached countries beyond the U.S. Thus Canada's share of world exports exclusive of the U.S. component is 1.2 per cent (instead of the overall figure of 4.5 per cent). Viewed differently, Canada's exports-to-GDP ratio exclusive of exports to the U.S. is only 6.7 per cent. A similar pattern characterizes Canadian FDI: 68 per cent of total CFDI is invested in the U.S., 7 per cent in the U.K. and 25 per cent in the rest of the world (Statistics Canada 1985).

It must be remembered that these statistics refer to Canada's overall performance, in line with the objectives of this study. Although the economy-wide data reflect low volumes and penetration rates, these can be very important on a regional or sectoral basis. For instance, wheat exports are, of course, a significant part of the Prairie provinces' economies; Saudi Arabia's telecommunications network has been developed almost exclusively by Canadian firms; and so on. On an aggregate basis, however, these niches do not negate Canada's overall low foreign penetration rates.

The main implication of the above is that Canada's presence in markets beyond North America, including the EC, is minimal indeed. Table V shows the relevant statistics and compares Canada to selected countries and regions. Coupled with the smaller base upon which these percentages are calculated for Canada (total exports of US$70 billion in 1982, or one-third, one-half, and one-seventh of U.S., Japanese, and EC exports respectively; see Table I), this means that Canada lacks a most essential ingredient that might allow further export development toward overseas destinations: a critical mass of Canadian products that would induce familiarity with, and further acceptance of, more exports and new products over time.

Viewed from the opposite angle, Canadian exports may be more likely to build upon the already strong base that exists in the U.S. than to develop from their presently insignificant status in other markets. This would imply increasing interdependence with the U.S. in trade and FDI, along the patterns established since the end of World War II. This fact gives rise to several policy questions that will be addressed in Chapter IV.

TABLE V. Exporter's Share in Imports

Importing Country	Total Imports	Exporter's Share in Imports of Importing Country (% 1982)				
		Exporting Country				
		EC-10	U.S.	Japan	Canada	World
EC-10	100	48.9[1]	8.5	2.9	1.0	38.7
U.S.	100	17.4	-	15.5	19.1	48.0
Japan	100	5.7	18.3	-	2.8	73.2
Canada	100	8.4	70.6	5.2	-	15.7

Note: (1) This percentage is intra-Community trade; if this is excluded, of course, EC's trade diversification is even broader.

Source: EUROSTAT, Basic Statistics of the Community; Edition 1984, Reference Period 1983.

2.3. *Exports and Investment in Manufactured Goods*

Another problem at the heart of the issue of Canada's relative international competitiveness is the deficit in manufactured goods. Unquestionably, the problem is often overstated and the important contribution of manufactured goods to Canadian exports frequently goes unmentioned (Astwood 1981:69). On the other hand, there is also no doubt that the export performance of the manufacturing sector overall has been weak.

The data in Table VI depict this weakness vividly. Thirteen of the 20 sectors that are listed are in a deficit position; the trade balance of 10 of these is deteriorating while that of the three other sectors has remained relatively stable over the past decade. The total deficit in manufactures became a net surplus in 1982 (mainly due to spectacular improvements in two sectors: Food and Beverages, and Transportation Equipment — mostly automobiles)[6], but then it moved back to a deficit position in 1984.

TABLE VI. Trade Balance in Canadian Manufacturing Sectors

SIC CODE	Sector	1976	1978	1980	1982	1984	Average 1966-1984	Surplus (+) or Deficit (−) Position	Improving (+) Stable (·) or Deteriorating (−)
500 0000	All Manufacturing	-4,141	-2,153	-1,792	3,690	-90	-1,795	−	:
501	Food and Beverages	35	281	709	1,374	896	436	+	+
502	Tobacco Products	-9	-10	-13	-22	-19	-9	−	:
503	Rubber and Plastics Products	-322	-491	-551	-187	-496	-329	−	:
504	Leather Industries	-288	-331	-374	-446	-684	-260	−	−
505	Textile Industries	-829	-968	-1,063	-988	-1,471	-773	−	−
506	Knitting Mills	-333	-306	-337	-366	-601	-249	−	−
507	Clothing Industries	-297	-217	-244	-390	-723	-200	−	−
508	Wood Industries	1,086	3,557	3,740	3,435	4,936	2,166	+	+
509	Furniture and Fixtures	-126	-123	-45	61	155	-35	+	+
510	Paper and Allied Industries	4,083	5,176	7,929	7,536	8,934	4,335	+	+
511	Printing and Publishing	-397	-555	-719	-884	-995	-465	−	−
512	Primary Metals Industries	2,108	2,913	4,272	3,420	4,427	2,074	+	+
513	Metal Fabricating Industries	-757	-883	-1,031	-912	-1,232	-677	−	−
514	Machinery Industries	-3,550	-4,300	-6,864	-5,729	-7,715	-3,641	−	−
515	Transportation Equipment	-945	-885	-2,401	2,738	2,679	-488	+	+
516	Electrical Products	-1,459	-1,910	-2,183	-2,144	-3,319	-1,397	−	−
517	Non-metallic Mineral Products	-311	-249	-444	-323	-357	-246	−	:
518	Petroleum and Coal Products	11	306	962	821	575	184	+	:
519	Chemical Products	-915	-939	-527	-517	-1,453	-665	−	−
520	Miscellaneous Manufacturing Industries	-1,528	-2,219	-2,609	-2,787	-3,626	-1,613	−	−

Source: Industry, Trade and Commerce and Regional Economic Expansion: Manufacturing Trade and Measures 1966-1984; Ottawa, August 1985.

Associated with the deficit issue is the very question of whether it should be worrisome at all, given Canada's strengths in agriculture and the resource sectors (Daly 1981a:704). Orthodox economic analysis has used the theory of comparative advantage to explain a country's relative strengths at the international level. Many economists in Canada argue that, at least for the short term, it would not be advisable to shift government support from agriculture and resources to manufacturing industries, for fear that this would weaken Canada's comparative advantage. For instance, the Economic Council of Canada has stated:

> "We consider ... that the facts do not justify policy emphasis on stimulating manufactured exports .... Such emphasis ... could create a production pattern that would lower real incomes in Canada. This would be the price for significantly moving away — unnecessarily, in our view — from the exploitation of our present comparative advantages in exporting" (1983: p. 128).

Yet, the importance of manufacturing in today's technology-based world and the need to increase the processing component of resources in exports in order to address problems such as unemployment and the current account deficit, would strongly point toward the opposite direction. In fact, as pointed out in 1981 by Michael Jenkins, a Science Council adviser, "the absence of support now ... [to manufacturing, is tantamount to] ... having to run twice as fast to stay in the same place later" (see also Science Council 1981).

The present differences between the manufacturing and other sectors, and the distance that the former would have to cover in order to begin to approach the comparative strength of the latter, are clearly exemplified through the ratio of implicit self-sufficiency of the main sectors in the Canadian economy. The relevant statistics are shown in Table VII. These show low levels of import penetration, and high levels of export orientation, for agriculture, fishing and trapping, and mining. This reflects the ability of these sectors to satisfy domestic needs while at the same time having the capacity to produce significant amounts of the respective commodities for export. The reverse is true in the case of manufacturing, where the implicit self-sufficiency ratio is significantly lower[7]. The ratio would, of course, be even lower for manufacturing were it not for automobile exports to the U.S. (see also Table VI).

TABLE VII. Self-Sufficiency, Import Penetration and Export Orientation[1]

	Import Penetration					Export Orientation					Implicit Self-Sufficiency				
	1966	1975	1978	1980	1982	1966	1975	1978	1980	1982	1966	1975	1978	1980	1982
All Goods Production	20.4	28.4	28.8	NA	NA	21.3	27.5	30.0	NA	NA	101.1	98.8	101.7	NA	NA
Economic Sectors:															
Agriculture	8.1	10.0	10.8	NA	NA	29.4	30.0	28.0	NA	NA	130.2	128.5	123.9	NA	NA
Forestry	1.9	2.6	2.1	NA	NA	4.4	1.9	1.6	NA	NA	102.6	99.3	99.5	NA	NA
Fishing/Trapping	2.7	10.5	8.0	NA	NA	32.6	36.2	33.4	NA	NA	144.3	140.3	138.0	NA	NA
Mining	28.3	49.6	34.6	NA	NA	47.2	62.9	47.3	NA	NA	135.8	135.8	124.1	NA	NA
Manufacturing	21.0	28.8	31.5	31.3	29.8	18.8	23.9	30.4	30.6	31.4	97.2	93.6	98.4	98.9	102.4

Note: (1) "Import Penetration": imports less re-exports/ Implicit Canadian Market
"Implicit Canadian Market": shipments plus imports less exports
"Export Orientation": domestic exports/shipments
"Implicit Self-sufficiency": shipments/ Implicit Canadian Market

Sources: for 1966-1978, Astwood 1981; for 1980-1982, "Manufacturing Trade and Measures 1966-1982", Industry, Trade and Commerce and Regional Economic Expansion, Ottawa, August 1983.

As far as CFDI is concerned, the pattern is again not much different from that of exports. A large proportion (48.6 per cent) of Canadian investment abroad is in manufacturing industries (reference year: 1978). This represents a decline from 52.7 per cent of the total in 1971. In the same period, Canada's stock of FDI in services also declined from 32.9 per cent to 28.6 per cent, while that in extractive industries rose from 14.4 per cent to 22.8 per cent (U.N. Centre on TNCs 1983). As at other points during the preceding discussion, these data are not cause for concern in and of themselves. They become so when compared with the corresponding data for Canada's major international competitors. The differences between Canada and other DMEs, in terms of the proportion of FDI in manufacturing vs. total, portray both Canada's strengths in relation to some major economies and its weaknesses in comparison to some of the newer entrants into the international investment sphere. For instance, Canada's ratio of outbound FDI in manufacturing vs. total FDI, at 48.6 per cent, is higher than those of Japan (34.2 per cent) and the U.S. (44.1 per cent) — but much lower than the ratios for West Germany and the Netherlands, at 69.5 per cent and 82.8 per cent, respectively (U.N. Centre on TNCs 1983:46-47).

As will be seen in Chapter III below, these general features of trade and investment in manufactures are clearly reflected in the Canada-EC relationship as well. Generally — and regardless of the detailed arguments that surround the manufactured exports and FDI question — an almost complete consensus appears to exist both in the literature and among those interviewed for this study: that Canada's future international competitiveness depends by and large on its ability to further strengthen its manufacturing sector.

3. Factors Affecting Canadian Trade and Foreign Investment

A key question that arises from the above discussion is: What are the main factors that have prevented Canadian industry from achieving higher levels of international activity, especially in manufacturing and outside North America? The answer has been the subject of numerous reports and heated arguments over the past few decades, and occupied a significant portion of the interviews in this study. Based on both, what follows is a brief summary of those issues that are especially relevant to the discussion of Canada-EC trade and investment patterns, as analysed in the following chapters.

3.1.   Policy Factors

Canadian federal and provincial policies concerning international trade and FDI have often been criticized as being erratic, ineffective, or inconsistent. While such criticism certainly does not apply to the entire policy spectrum, there are enough examples to support it at least to a certain extent, and especially in the context of Canada's economic relationship with the Community and its member states. A non-exhaustive list would include:

a.   The perceived inconsistency between a pro-internationalist view on outward trade and investment on the one hand, and protectionist policies on the other. The (now abolished) National Energy Program and Foreign Investment Review Agency, the continuation of quotas on a variety of products (e.g. textiles and footwear), relatively high tariffs, and both federal and provincial non-tariff barriers, are among those measures which have attracted significant attention in the recent past[8].

b.   The vascillation between various countries or regions as possible policy targets for trade development (see below).

c.   The relative lack of support for Canadian manufactured exports, especially in view of the heavy subsidies offered by other governments (e.g. France and other European countries in, for example, the telecommunications sector) to their domestic industries (e.g. see Voyer and Murphy 1984).

d.   The frequent unwillingness of federal agencies to finance exports indirectly through government-to-government loans, which would help pull Canadian products into foreign markets (Barrows and Lyman 1975; see also The Citizen 2-11-81).

e.   Finally, the lack of encouragement for and low spending proportion on research and development (Science Council 1984).

Some of these policies have had noticeable effects on Canada's external economic relationship with industrialized countries outside of North America and more specifically on transatlantic investment and trade flows. Two sample cases may be highlighted here. FIRA was a prime example of both inconsistency and ineffectiveness in policy-making. On the one hand, the agency was established at precisely the point in time when Canada was actively lobbying the international community for increased liberalization and reduced protectionism in both trade and foreign investments (1974). On the other hand, although it was in practice, at worst, a rather benevolent barrier to inward FDI, it managed to be perceived as a clear "enemy" by foreign investors.

It is interesting to note that fully 85 per cent of the 2,860 applications that were received by FIRA between 1974-1980 were approved, the remainder being either withdrawn or disallowed in roughly equal proportions. Further, Dewhirst (1981) shows that one in four of the disallowed applications was eventually resubmitted, and almost all (88 per cent) of the re-applications were approved. Yet interviews with both government and industry officials made it clear that the agency was perceived in Europe as a much more serious barrier than the above statistics show. Similar views were found to prevail in a 1983 Conference Board study of foreign investors (mainly from the U.S.) about the investment climate in Canada (Beckman 1984). As a result, instead of potentially screening out applications that might not have been deemed beneficial for Canada, it is widely believed that FIRA simply had the effect of inadvertently preventing many foreign investors (mostly from countries outside of North America) from ever submitting applications to invest in Canada.

The second example which is relevant to this discussion is the different emphasis placed by various Canadian trade policies at different times upon different regions of the world. Dolan (1978) has shown that Canada has traditionally used Western Europe as a counterweight to its close relationship with the U.S. The question of whether Canada should move toward even stronger economic ties with the U.S. has emerged and then subsided several times during the nation's history. A good summary of this issue can be found in Reisman (1984), who has made the point, among others, that:

> "Canadian interest in reciprocity [with the U.S.] traditionally has peaked during periods of economic difficultly or when Canada has been frustrated by difficulties with other trading partners, particularly the United Kingdom and Western Europe" (p. 43).

The most recent case in point is the shift from the pro-diversification "Third Option" policy of the early 1970s to the present emphasis on a comprehensive free trade agreement with the U.S. The aim of that policy was to develop a "comprehensive long-term strategy" that would result in diversifying Canadian external trade and in reducing "the present Canadian vulnerability [to the U.S.]" (Sharp 1972; Munton and Swanson 1978). One of the manifestations of the pro-diversification mood of that period was the signing of a Framework Agreement for a "contractual link" between Canada and the EC in 1976.

In retrospect, this agreement and the policy that spawned it are widely perceived as failures. As early as 1976, former Conservative party leader Robert Stanfield called it a "big bag of fog", and *The Economist* scorned it as a "hitherto unknown animal that goes by the name of a 'contractual link'" (see Gwyn 1981:302; Dolan 1978:26). By 1981 *The Globe and Mail* was concluding that the very phrase "third option" had become an "embarrassment" (Lukaciewicz 1981). Finally, in 1985, the Macdonald Royal Commission on the Economic Union and Development Prospects for Canada recommended free trade with the U.S. (also making reference to the absence of results from the Third Option; Macdonald Royal Commission 1985:18); this had been the Second (and rejected) Option presented by the federal government during the earlier deliberations of 1972.

As already noted, this recommendation was adopted and the federal government announced its intention to attempt to reach a free trade agreement with the U.S. In the "Quebec Declaration", following the March 18, 1985, summit meeting between Prime Minister Brian Mulroney and President Ronald Reagan, the two leaders agreed to commence the discussion process, with the aim of developing such a bilateral agreement (Canadian Trade Negotiations 1985).

A large part of the failure of the diversification policy may be attributed to unfavourable world economic conditions in the late 1970s, the rise in the value of the Canadian dollar against European currencies over the past few years, and other systemic factors. However, many of the respondents in this study pointed out that the policy also failed because of its vague objectives that were never sufficiently operationalized, because of the lack of the political will to implement it, and because it never enjoyed wide support beyond a small circle of policy makers in the government of that time. In point of fact, most of the European and many Canadian respondents in this study expressed the view that the short-lived drive toward diversification — never seriously pursued — may have been a delayed result of Canadian euphoria over a strong economy in the late 1960s-early 1970s, which fostered a spirit of independence — and which faltered once the economic climate worsened (see also Reisman 1984:43f).

An alternate view on the same point suggests that:

"Canadian policy makers pursue increased continental integration during periods of growth in the American economy and when Canada's trade and investment ties are less exclusively concentrated with the United States [and vice versa]" (von Riekhoff and Tomlin 1984:160-161).

However, the *exact direction* of Canadian policy in relation to the strength of the North American economy is perhaps less important than the apparent fact that the former is shaped on the basis of conditions in the latter. Although the above views suggest alternative explanations as to whether integrationist vs. diversification policies follow a strong or a weak North American economy, they agree on one point: that Canadian trade policy is, to a large extent, a function of whether Canadian governments feel sufficiently strong to either negotiate with, or stray away from, the United States.

This, of course, can be seen as nothing but economic pragmatism. Yet, what may appear domestically as justifiable vacillation because of prevailing economic conditions, results in an outward image, such as that held about Canada in Europe, of inconsistent foreign trade policy. Ultimately, Canada can ill afford friction with its major trading partners – whether Western Europe, the U.S., or Japan – resulting from swings between the search for understanding in times of weakness, on the one hand, and complacency in times of strength, on the other (see also Daly 1981b:14).

3.2. Structural Issues in International Performance

Partially as a result of policy and partially because of the small size of the Canadian economy, the country's geographic position and other factors, Canadian industry has several unique characteristics which affect its ability to compete effectively in the international sphere. As in earlier sections, it is beyond the scope of this essay to discuss all of these characteristics. Four of these, however, are particularly relevant to Canadian exports and investments toward the EC and will be discussed here.

3.2.1. Foreign Ownership in Canadian Industry

The subject of foreign ownership in Canadian industry has been at the forefront of economic debate over several decades (e.g. see Crookell 1985; Banner 1979; Safarian 1971; Rostein 1976; Hurtig 1979). Unfortunately, many of the critics on either side have failed to "explore the full range of questions that can be based on *existing* data" (emphasis added; Britton and Gilmour 1978:21). This last statement becomes especially relevant in the context of a realization that emerged in the course of conducting the research for the present study. This refers to the fact that, regardless of their nationality, foreign corporations are important actors in Canada's foreign trade and tend to influence it through their individual and collective decisions and operations.

One of the key characteristics of inward FDI is that many of the investing enterprises tend to select Canada on the strength of its main comparative advantage (i.e. resources) rather than because of its technological strength (which, in many cases, is equally available at home). A main reason behind such investments is the need to secure a reliable supply of resources for export to the parent firm, where they are used in the production of fully manufactured products.

International companies from resource-hungry Japan and from the geographically-convenient U.S. invest mainly in low-technology, low labour-intensive sectors such as resources and primary manufacturing (with the obvious exception of the automotive and a few other sectors; see Litvak 1984:xix; Wright 1984); they import higher-technology products (e.g. machinery and equipment) from their parent firms; and their locus of ownership (hence their export destination) is more often than not the U.S. and, often replacing European investors, Japan (Banner 1979; Gherson, Gratton and McMillan 1979; Wright 1984).

What is relevant to this discussion is not whether or not such investments are beneficial to Canada domestically, but rather, their effect on its trade. Of Canada's 50 largest exporters, 19 are foreign owned and controlled (by 51 per cent or more) and another three are partly owned by foreign investors. Of these, 14 companies are mainly in resource extractive industries and only eight are in manufacturing (four of these are General Motors, Chrysler, Ford, and American Motors; see *Financial Post* 1984). Further, approximately three-quarters of Canadian imports are brought in by foreign-owned firms, most of it by U.S. multinational companies (Statistics Canada; see also Economic Council 1983). Finally, nine Japanese trading companies (two of which are included in the above-mentioned 19) accounted for about $5 billion of Canadian trade in 1980; this amounted to 71 per cent of all exports and 41 per cent of all imports of Canada to and from Japan (Wright 1984:xix).

The conclusions that can be derived from the above three paragraphs can go a long way towards explaining the nature and structure of Canadian trade, as these were described in the preceding pages. In this sense, the nature and origin of most foreign investment in Canada appears to be a key factor in helping to concentrate Canadian trade in two of the slowest-growing areas: resources, in sectoral terms, and the U.S., insofar as destinations are concerned. The dangers arising from this "specialization", and the need to strengthen both Canada's offshore presence and manufactured exports, have been discussed extensively by several researchers (see, for example, Beckman 1982:23 and Daly 1982:15).

The remaining three issues that help explain Canada's international performance in structural terms flow from two basic causes: the effects of foreign ownership on trade and the size of the Canadian economy.

3.2.2. Small Indigenous Firms

Fully 28 per cent of Canada's 50 largest industrial corporations, 37 per cent of the largest 200, 42.5 per cent of the largest 400, and 40 per cent of the largest 500 are totally or majority-owned by foreign parents (another 22 among the top 500 are minority-controlled; *Financial Post* 1984). In addition, of those Canadian firms that are listed in the *Fortune 500 Largest Non-US. Industrials* "list, only about half are Canadian-controlled.

These figures clearly indicate the comparatively small number of large indigenous firms in the Canadian market and, by exclusion, the fact that the majority of Canadian firms are too small to be included in the above lists. These statistics can also be viewed in relation to empirical findings which show that the smaller the firm, the less likely it is to engage in exports and the more likely, if it does, it is to seek geographically and culturally "near" markets (Welch and Wiedersheim-Paul 1980; Crookell and Caliendo 1980; Kaynak 1981). Taken together, these points also help explain the U.S. concentration and low export orientation of the technology-intensive, but small in size, component of Canadian manufacturing.

3.2.3. Corporate Identity

The second issue stems from the international behaviour of Canadian multinational enterprises. As Rugman has shown (1985) many Canadian MNCs have successfully internalized the country-specific advantages that Canada offers, being thus able to grow and become formidable competitors in foreign markets. On the other hand, many of the respondents in this study pointed to a rather unique phenomenon that seems to characterize the behaviour of successful Canadian multinational enterprises.

This phenomenon can be described in broad terms as follows: in line with traditional patterns, the majority of outward FDI by Canadian multinational companies (MNCs) is concentrated in the U.S.; given the large size of the U.S. and the small size of the Canadian markets, the U.S. operations become, more often than not, larger than their parents. When further investment outside North America is next contemplated, many of these firms choose to undertake it from their American, rather than Canadian base; the combined size of the U.S.-located and U.S.-run investments then makes the American subsidiary even larger than before, compared with its parent. In the next natural step, the parent often moves many (if not most) of the headquarters' functions to the seat of its subsidiary. Coupled with the frequent inability of both the subsidiary and the parent to source manufactured materials in Canada for export to foreign operations[9], the above results in the gradual loss of identity of the original Canadian corporation which, for all practical purposes, becomes a U.S. firm.

Although it is extremely difficult to quantify questions of corporate identity, and although this subject has received only little attention in the literature, some data from the Litvak and Maule studies on Canadian MNCs tend to support the above contention (1981:32). Rugman (1984) also addresses this issue briefly while also citing examples of other corporations which have maintained a strong Canadian identity.

The phenomenon of sales to large foreign markets exceeding those to small domestic ones is common, but the loss of identity is not. In the case of Canadian firms, this may be due to the presence of another dominant identity, the U.S., which can in turn be attributed to the large concentration of CFDI in that country. By contrast, MNCs from other small countries (e.g. Sweden, Switzerland, the Netherlands) tend to maintain their identity at least partially because their investments are spread more widely throughout the world.

3.2.4. Tariff Protection

The third and final subject that will be addressed here, in the context of the structural issues that may be affecting the level of international activity of Canadian industry, is the impact on size and competitiveness of the tariff protection that has been afforded to many manufacturing sectors. This issue has been discussed extensively in the literature (e.g. see Sweeney 1980; Anderson 1981) and does not need to be elaborated upon here. Crookell and Caliendo (1980:58) have perhaps summarized the essence of the question in a most succinct manner:

> "Secondary industry in Canada has long been plagued by higher insular tariffs ... [with the firm] often pricing up to the limit of tariff protection because of the high cost of small diversified production".

Stated simply, in a tariff-protected market there exists little incentive for manufacturers to develop internationally competitive products based on innovation, economies of scale and the like. This is especially so in Canada where the manufacturing sector's shortcomings are masked by substantial commodity trade surpluses. Canadian (and other) tariffs have, of course, been reduced substantially in recent years as a result of successive rounds of negotiation at the General Agreement of Tariffs and Trade (GATT; see Stone 1984). Nonetheless, the problem persists, to a large extent, because several key industries (e.g. textiles, clothing, ships, rail cars) have been partially exempted and Canada has supplemented its tariff protection with import quotas for some of these products, as well as for a range of agricultural goods.

3.3. Other Factors in Canada's International Competitiveness

In addition to the preceding issues, which could be broadly grouped under the policy and structure headings, there exist several other factors that have impeded Canada's ability to develop a more competitive foreign presence, especially in manufacturing. Three of these are related to the decline in Canadian-European Community trade and need to be discussed briefly.

The first is the relative lack of a sufficient number of adequately trained personnel in those key areas that might have a positive effect on industrial management and competitiveness. As Peter Drucker once observed, "Management is the central resource of the developed countries". In the technology-oriented societies of the 1980s and beyond, the same can be said of engineering, research, and other functional specialties in industry. Yet Canada has been traditionally deficient in all three areas. For instance, the U.S. produced three times as many MBA graduates as Canada on a per capita basis in 1981, and government reports estimate the shortfall in qualified engineers and researchers at about 12,000 and 4,500 respectively (see Witten 1981; *Citizen* 23-12-1981 and 15-05-1985).

Related to this problem, and in fact aggravating its effects, is the next issue, which refers to the composition and nature of available managerial personnel in Canadian industry. Many of the interviewees in this study expressed the opinion that Canadian business people have traditionally been more capable as administrators than as managers. The literature is filled with references by various researchers who confirm this opinion. For instance:

"The business community has been slow at times to recognize attractive opportunities for [international] diversification because of the habit of tapping accustomed sources of capital and of dealing with familiar markets". (von Riekhoff 1978:100).

"Involved ... [in the ability to penetrate foreign markets] ... is the need for managerial commitment to product innovation and international marketing, a commitment for which the past strategies of most firms have not prepared them". (Crookell and Caliendo 1980:59).

"Unfortunately, most managers of ... [earlier generations] ... will not be remembered for their initiative, innovation, imagination, or international outlook. They tended to be conservative administrators with an inordinate respect for authority ...". (Witten 1981:15).

Compared with the aggressive and marketing-oriented American, Swedish, or French business people (Henry 1981), or to the reputation, at least in Canada, of the Japanese as being "highly aggressive ... in their business dealings" (Wright 1984), Canadian managers still appear to be more comfortable with the traditional "trading" mode in international business, rather than with the contemporary "marketing" mode. The difference between the two is substantial and can have a significant impact on the international modus operandi of the individual firm.

"Trading" is used here in the sense of large-scale, often government-supported transactions, which are grounded firmly on a unique and country-specific comparative advantage. Conversely, "marketing" is used to connote a host of contemporary competencies which, as has been pointed out, are generally missing from indigenous Canadian industry. These include the ability of the firm to develop competitive (rather than "comparative" in the traditional sense; see also Note 4, Chapter I) advantages through product innovation and international market positioning, and to develop strengths based on what industry can *do* (knowledge and technology) rather than on what it may *own* (resources; see Papadopoulos 1982a:230)[10].

As with other subjects that were discussed in these pages, the third and final issue that has had an effect on Canada's international competitiveness is inter-related with the preceding ones. This refers to the nature rather than the level of government assistance programs for the internationalization of the individual Canadian firm. Some of the better known assistance programs include PEMDE (Program for Export Market Development), the EDC (Export Development Corporation), CTTF (Canadian Technology Transfer Facility) and the Trade Commissioner posts at Canadian Embassies abroad, along with their provincial counterparts in many foreign countries (including several cities in the U.S., as well as France, West Germany, the U.K., and elsewhere). Coupled with the development of, and pivotal role assigned to, many Crown corporations, some of these programs (though certainly not all) have tended to substitute for, rather than assist, the development of international business and marketing expertise on the part of Canadian industry (Papadopoulos 1982a:141).

This tendency has in turn created two distinct but related problems: on the one hand, it has found easy acceptance within administratively-inclined Canadian management, thus retarding the development of Canadian entrepreneurship. On the other hand, it has occupied government resources in areas where it lacks expertise, rather than channelling them into effective programs which might have had a more immediate and positive impact on Canadian trade. As a result, effective trade vehicles such as the Japanese- or American-modelled trading houses, the Italian model of foreign trade institutes, and others, have often been the subject of policy discussion but, just as often, have been put on the back burner and never implemented.

3.4. Recent Developments in Canadian External Economic Policies

Several initiatives, concerning Canada's economic relations with its major partners, have recently been undertaken by both the federal and some provincial governments. These may be classified in four general categories:

a. The opening of trade talks with the United States, aimed at removing remaining barriers to investment and trade through a bilateral agreement;

b. Canada's support for a new round of multilateral trade negotiations under the auspices of the GATT;

c. Policies aimed at encouraging foreign direct investments in Canada;

d. Provincial initiatives tailored to foster external trade and investment in sectors or with regions that are of particular interest to individual provinces. These include the Ontario government's extensive support program for the high technology industry, Quebec's efforts to forge closer links with Francophone nations world-wide, and British Columbia's view of the 1986 World Fair (Expo 86) as, among others, an instrument in opening a gateway for trade with Pacific Rim countries.

Such policies are certainly more in line with Canada's outward pro-trade philosophy. It is, of course, still too early to assess their impact or forecast their longevity. Information about them is still limited largely to formal announcements about the new policies (e.g. see "Canadian Trade Negotiations" 1985; The Right Hon. Joe Clark 1985) and to numerous discussions and reports in the mass media. Nonetheless, these initiatives will be referred to, where necessary, in the discussion that follows, since they are likely to have a significant impact on Canada's future trade and investment patterns.

Notes

1. The relevant statistics appear in Table I. Note, however, that these are based on IMF's "Direction of Trade", which expresses trade in U.S. dollars. Instead, the European Community's EUROSTAT, reporting for the same years in ECUs (devalued relative to the U.S. dollar) shows an increase in world exports from 1.768 trillion ECUs in 1981 to 2.027 trillion in 1983 (Basic Statistics of the Community; Edition 1984, Ref. period 1983).

2. Norvel and Raveed (1980) have identified 11 distinct factors behind the drive toward internationalization on the part of individual business firms: fleeing recessions, countering demographic changes, extending product life cycles, and keeping up with or escaping competition; adjusting to new technologies and creating new research opportunities; obtaining more political clout and establishing a progressive image; achieving economies of scale and disposing of excess inventories; and enjoying tax advantages.

3. A 1967 United Nations resolution, strongly recommending a switch from import substitution to export development as the preferred method for industrialization, was one of the factors that encouraged the spreading of this attitude across the less developed world. That resolution resulted in the establishment of numerous Export Processing Zones, the development of new forms of (and demands for)

countertrade, and other measures which helped bring countries such as South Korea, Taiwan, and Singapore to the forefront of international trade (Jayawardena 1983; UNCTAD 1983; Papadopoulos 1985).

4. The only other developed market economies that showed export growth between 1982 and 1983 were Japan, Denmark, Ireland, Norway and Sweden (source: IMF-Direction of Trade).

5. The concentration of Canadian trade and FDI in the U.S. can be seen both as a strength and as a weakness. The extent of the penetration of Canadian firms in the U.S. market, which is the most saturated and competitive one in the world, is certainly impressive, and exports to the U.S. form an integral and important part of the Canadian economy. Most researchers agree, however, that in proportionate terms this volume reflects too high levels of concentration and interdependence among the two economies. This view is shared, at least implicitly, by those who favour "continentalism" since few, if any, propose integration with the U.S. to the *exclusion* of overall diversification.

6. The source for the data in Table IV is "Manufacturing Trade and Measures 1966-1984", prepared by the Department of Regional Industrial Expansion. It suggests some caution in using these data because they are subject to noise due to the various methods used in deriving export, import, and shipment statistics. Since this discussion focuses on comparisons among sectors and across years, rather than on analyzing the absolute values of specific sectors in specific years, the potential problems of the data have no effect on the conclusions reached here.

7. The ratio of "implicit self-sufficiency" is used here only as a gross measure of comparative strength across sectors. It does not, by any means, imply that "self-sufficiency" (in the isolationist sense) would be a desirable objective.

8. A number of policy changes have been implemented recently reflecting the greater emphasis placed on market forces by the present Progressive Conservative government in Canada. Besides terminating the National Energy Program, the new administration replaced FIRA with a

much less restrictive agency, "Investment Canada" (whose mandate, in fact, includes the attraction of suitable inward investment), eliminated most import quotas on shoes (but not yet on clothing and textiles), and announced its intention to privatize several Crown corporations which used to enjoy special protection or subsidies.

9.   The suggestion that Canadian multinationals and turn-key engineering firms are frequently unable to source manufactured products in Canada to cover their offshore needs raises vehement protests and objections in some quarters. Although references to this effect in the literature are scant (e.g. see Litvak and Maule 1981:73), this subject was frequently brought up by interviewees in this study. Most vocal among them were the marketing director of a major Canadian MNC in the energy sector, and executives from two different telecommunications firms. The first case concerned pipes of a particular diameter and strength, and the second was about plastic casings for telephone devices. In both cases, the interviewees claimed that they had been unable to source the appropriate materials in Canada, in spite of substantial assistance offered by various government departments.

10.   That paper (Papadopoulos 1982a:230) makes reference to the difference between comparative advantage based on "competence" instead of on "possession". That concept, and its importance to Canada, have also been elaborated upon more recently by Crookell (1985:103) who uses the terms "wealth-by-effort" and "wealth-by-right", respectively.

Chapter II:

The European Community in International Trade

"The European Community has not created a 'United States of Europe' or even a full economic union — but who had a right to expect that?"
W. Diebold
1968

As was mentioned in the Introduction, the European Community can be considered as a large experiment in economic and political integration, unlike any other in recent history. Perhaps one of its most significant accomplishments to date, in view of the multiplicity of cultures, national interests, past enmities, and future aspirations which it blends, is that it has not failed yet—and is not expected to in the foreseeable future. The Community has been successful in creating a unique and large free trade area which helped the economies of its member states and made them evolve, collectively, into the largest trading block in the world. Further, it has created an even larger network of free trade arrangements with neighbouring countries in Western Europe and the Mediterranean area, as well as with the former colonies of its members.

Because of the enormity of this undertaking and of its immediate and potential implications in world affairs, the EC has been studied almost exhaustively from every conceivable angle by countless researchers around the globe (although, as already mentioned, there is a dearth of publications examining specifically bilateral Canadian-EC economic issues). Individual publications have dealt with EC-related subjects ranging from political integration and economic co-operation to the development of transnational corporate law and the role of international institutions.

This extensive coverage of EC issues makes it unnecessary to re-address them here[1]. Instead, the purpose of this chapter is to briefly discuss three important issues that are of direct relevance to Canada's trade with the Community: the nature of and trends in EC trade, both internally and with non-EC countries; the network of links and associations between the Community's member states and other countries; and the present

37

status and future role of the EC from a general, global perspective. Using this and the previous chapter as background, the third chapter will then consider specifically Canadian-EC trade and investment questions.

1.   Community Trade and Foreign Investment

The nature of and trends in EC trade are depicted in four tables. Table VIII compares the growth of trade of the EC, its member states, Canada, the U.S., Japan, the U.S.S.R. and the "Rest of World" countries in terms of both imports and exports between 1968 and 1983. Table IX shows merchandise origins and destinations for the same countries and regions, along with their trade-to-GDP ratios. Table X contains a sectoral breakdown of imports and exports. Finally, Table XI includes trade balance statistics up to January 1985.

Taken together, these four tables provide a rather comprehensive picture of EC trade. The following comments highlight some of its key elements:

a.   EC trade, both among its members and externally, grew tremendously over the past two decades. While it slowed down to world-wide growth levels in the last few years, it maintained a fast growth rate until 1979. In fact, EC trade growth outpaced all other DMEs in the period leading to 1975. As a result, the EC now accounts for over 30 per cent of world imports and exports (Table VIII).

b.   As already mentioned, EC trade is well diversified. About half of the member states' trade is accounted for by intra-EC flows, while another 39 per cent of their imports and exports originate in or are destined to countries outside of the main trading entities of the EC itself, the U.S., and Japan. As well, the Community accounts for 13 per cent of imports by, and for 18 per cent of exports from, the Soviet Union (Table IX).

c.   On a sectoral basis, imports are fairly diversified between basic resources and manufactured goods, their distribution being not much unlike that of Canada and the U.S. On the other hand, EC exports are heavily concentrated in the machinery, equipment, and other end-product sectors — much like those of the U.S. but less so than Japan's and more so than Canada's (Table X).

d.   Finally, Table XI shows that over the past few years, the general conditions that have characterized the balance of trade of the major OECD economies, including the EC, have remained largely unchanged — with three exceptions: the

TABLE VIII. Imports and Exports of the EC, Canada, and Other Selected Countries

	Total Imports						Total Exports					
	Imports (billion ECUs)[1]			Growth Rate 1975 = 100		Imports as % of EC total (1983)	Exports (billion ECUs)			Growth Rate 1975 = 100		Exports as % of EC total (1983)
Country	1968	1975	1983	1968	1983		1968	1975	1983	1968	1983	
Belgium + Luxembourg	8	25	62	32	248	9.3	8	23	58	35	252	9.0
Denmark	3	8	19	38	238	2.9	3	7	18	43	257	2.8
West Germany	20	60	171	33	285	25.7	25	73	190	34	260	29.5
Greece	1	4	11	25	275	1.7	0.5	2	5	25	250	0.1
France	14	44	118	32	268	17.7	13	42	103	31	245	16.0
Ireland	1	3	10	33	333	1.5	1	3	10	33	333	1.6
Italy	10	31	90	32	290	13.5	10	28	82	36	293	12.7
Netherlands	9	28	69	32	246	10.4	8	29	74	28	255	11.5
United Kingdom	19	43	114	44	265	17.1	15	35	105	43	300	16.3
EC-10	87	247	666	35	270	100.0	84	241	645	35	268	100.0

	Imports (billion ECUs)[1]			Growth Rate 1975 = 100		Imports as % of World total (1983)	Exports (billion ECUs)			Growth Rate 1975 = 100		Exports as % of World total (1983)
	1968	1975	1983	1968	1983		1968	1975	1983	1968	1983	
EC-10	–	–	–	–	–	31.8	–	–	–	–	–	31.8
Canada	12	27	69	44	255	3.3	13	26	83	50	319	4.1
U.S.	33	78	290	42	372	13.8	35	87	225	40	259	11.1
Japan	13	47	142	28	302	6.8	13	45	165	29	367	8.1
U.S.S.R.	9	30	90	30	300	4.3	11	27	103	41	381	5.1
World	234	729	2096	32	288	100.0	223	705	2027	32	288	100.0

Note: All imports c.i.f. (except Canada and the U.S. f.o.b.), all exports f.o.b.
(1) ECU: European Currency Unit
Source: EUROSTAT, Basic Statistics of the Community, Editions 1984 and 1978 (Ref. periods 1983 and 1976).

TABLE IX. Origins, Destinations and Importance of World Trade

Country	Total	Import Origins (1983-%)				Export Destinations (1983-%)				Trade-to-GDP (1983-%)	
		EC-10	U.S.	Japan	Rest of World	EC-10	U.S.	Japan	Rest of World	Imports	Exports
Belgium + Lux.	100	64	7	2	27	70	5	1	24	69	62
Denmark	100	49	6	3	43	48	8	2	42	30	28
W. Germany	100	50	7	4	40	48	8	1	43	24	27
Greece	100	48	4	7	42	53	6	1	41	26	11
France	100	53	7	2	38	49	6	1	43	21	17
Ireland	100	72	13	3	12	69	8	2	21	55	46
Italy	100	43	6	1	50	46	8	1	45	25	21
Netherlands	100	53	9	2	35	72	4	1	23	46	48
U.K.	100	43	14	5	38	44	14	1	41	22	21
EC-10	100	50	8	3	39	52	8	1	39	26	25
Canada	100	7	72	6	15	7	73	5	15	18	23
U.S.	100	16	-	16	69	20	-	11	69	8	7
Japan	100	6	20	-	75	12	30	-	59	12	13
U.S.S.R.	100	13	3	4	80	18	0.4	2	80	NA	NA
World	100	33	13	9	46	34	15	7	41	- -	- -

Source: IMF Direction of Trade Statistics, Annual Yearbook, 1984, for World data.
EUROSTAT, Basic Statistics of the Community, Edition 1984, Ref. Period 1983 for all other data.

TABLE X. Composition of Trade

SITC CODE	Food, beverages, tobacco (0+1)	Mineral fuels, lubricants, and related (3)	Crude materials, oils, fats (2+4)	Machinery, equipment (7)	Other (5+6+8+9)	Total
Country						
Imports (1983-%)						
EC-10	11.5	21.4	7.0	23.5	36.6	100
Canada	6.6	6.8	5.1	50.5	31.0	100
U.S.	7.3	22.5	3.9	33.4	33.0	100
Japan	11.8	42.6	14.4	7.4	19.6	100
Exports (1983-%)						
EC-10	10.5	9.4	3.3	33.0	43.9	100
Canada	11.5	14.1	14.7	33.9	25.9	100
U.S.	13.5	4.7	10.0	41.2	30.6	100
Japan	1.0	0.3	0.9	57.9	39.9	100

Source: EUROSTAT, Basic Statistics of the Community, Edition 1984, Ref. Period 1983; based on Standard International Trade Classification, Rev.2.

TABLE XI. Recent Trends in Balance of Trade
(monthly averages – million U.S.$)

Country/Region	1982	1983	1984	1985 [1]
OECD	-5467	-4872	-7980 [2]	NA
EC-10	-2267	-1413	-1494 [2]	NA
of which:				
West Germany	1784	1403	1583	1634
United Kingdom	- 205	- 690	- 912	- 808
France	-1919	-1148	- 861	-1022
Netherlands	304	334	306	NA
Canada	1133	1040	1072	867
United States	-2640	-4793	-8986	-7917
Japan	594	1717	2800	4071

Notes: (1) January
(2) first nine months' average
All exports f.o.b., all imports c.i.f. (except U.S. and
Canadian imports f.o.b.)

Source: OECD, Main Economic Indicators, April 1985

improvement in France's deficit position in comparison to 1982;
the significant improvement in Japan's surplus in each of the
past three years, continuing into 1985; and the deterioration in
the U.S. deficit, fuelled as it has been by the continuing strength
of the American dollar internationally.

In terms of foreign investment, the Community's strength
both as investor and as host of foreign investment was already
noted in the Introduction and in Table II. More recent statistics
on U.S. FDI show that Western Europe continues to be a
preferred region for investment by American firms (although, on
a country-by-country basis, Canada is still host to the largest
proportion of American FDI). Table XII shows that six European
countries (five EC and one non-EC) accounted for 32 per cent of
U.S. FDI stocks as of 1981, while Western Europe as a whole
accounted for 44 per cent of the total. This is the result of a 53 per

cent growth rate of investments in Europe between 1975-1980, which outpaced the growth of U.S. investment in almost every other region, including Canada.

TABLE XII. Distribution of U.S. FDI

Destination	Total FDI (1981-billion US$)	Distribution (%)	% Change, 1975-80
France	9	4	48
West Germany	16	7	48
Italy	5	2	50
United Kingdom	30	13	55
Spain*	3	1	48
EC-5	63	27	NA
Switzerland	12	5	59
Other Western Europe	26	11	NA
Total Western Europe	101	44	53
Canada	47	21	36
Africa	7	3	39
Middle East	2	1	3
Latin America	39	17	49
Asia	18	8	47
Australasia	9	4	38
Other	4	2	26
Total Other	126	56	NA
Total	227	100	44

* Spain joined the EC in 1986.

Source: Business International, "Competitive Strategies for Europe", July 1983.

It is also interesting to note the comparative position of the
EC in foreign investments through the number of firms involved,
rather than through the value of FDI stock. Although it is
somewhat dated by now, a comprehensive 1976 study of 9,481
multinational companies (MNC) clearly shows the origins of the
rising importance of European MNCs, which was to result in the
"end of U.S. dominance" that was discussed earlier (Ch.I.1; see
Franco 1978). That study showed that fully 48 per cent of those
MNCs were based in the EC. These companies accounted for 56
per cent of the total number of links (subsidiaries, associated
companies, or trade investments) by all of the world's MNCs.
Finally, the study showed the EC to be the largest host region for
MNC links world-wide, accounting for 41 per cent of the total, or
for 36,351 external MNC links (Survey 1976).

2.   External Associations of the EC

More important than the actual statistics for trade and
investment, as far as this study is concerned, is the Community's
development of a large number of association or co-operation
agreements on trade and related areas with numerous countries
around the world. Some of the major agreements are outlined
briefly below.

2.1. EFTA

The European Free Trade Association includes six non-EC West
European countries (Austria, Finland, Iceland, Norway, Sweden,
and Switzerland). EFTA was established in 1960; the original
membership included the U.K., Denmark, and Portugal, which
left to join the EC (the first two in 1973, Portugal in 1986), but
not Finland and Iceland, which became members in 1961 and
1970 respectively.

Of special importance here are the 1972 free trade
agreements between the Community and EFTA's member
countries, implemented gradually over the years until they came
fully in force in 1984 (Lugon 1985; *The Globe and Mail* 27-05-
1985:R3). These agreements have resulted in the creation of a
European free trade system, containing all the EFTA and EC
members. Although some products (e.g. agriculture) are
excluded or subject to special provisions and arrangements, the
system applies to most industrial goods. EFTA states account for
nearly 15 per cent of each other's trade, while the EC accounts for
54 per cent and 52 per cent respectively of EFTA's imports and
exports. Table XIII shows the relevant statistics and highlights
two important points: first, the growth in intra-EFTA trade since

TABLE XIII. EFTA Trade: Trends and Main Partners

Year	EFTA	EC-10	Canada (a)	U.S.	Japan	Eastern Europe	Other	World
1. Imports from- (billion US$)								
1972	5	18	NA	2	1	2	4	32
1982	15	61	0.7	9	5	9	15	115
1983	14	59	0.7	8	5	9	14	110
2. Exports to- (billion US$)								
1972	5	13	NA	2	0.4	2	5	27
1982	15	53	0.8	6	1	7	21	104
1983	15	54	0.9	7	2	7	18	104
3. Shares of- in EFTA imports (%)								
1959	9	59	NA	9	1	7	15	100
1972	16	57	NA	6	3	5	13	100
1982	13	53	0.6	7	4	8	14	100
1983	13	54	0.6	8	4	8	12	100
4. Shares of- in EFTA exports (%)								
1959	11	51	NA	9	1	8	20	100
1972	19	49	NA	7	1	6	18	100
1982	14	51	0.8	6	1	7	20	100
1983	14	52	0.9	7	2	7	17	100

Notes: EFTA established 1960; U.K. and Denmark left in 1973, Portugal in 1986 to join the EC: Finland joined EFTA in 1961, Iceland in 1970; present membership includes Austria, Norway, Sweden, Finland, Switzerland, Iceland.

(a) estimate based on first semester (1982 and 1983).

Source: European Free Trade Association, "EFTA Trade-1983", March 1985

its creation; second, the success of the EC and EFTA countries in maintaining a strong trade partnership between 1959 and today.

2.2. ACP

The EC concluded three treaties between 1976 and 1984 with a large number of African, Caribbean and Pacific nations – the so-called ACP countries.   The treaties give free EC access to practically all products from ACP countries and are known as Lome I, II and III. The latest treaty incorporates 76 ACP nations, many of which were former colonies of France, the U.K., Belgium, the Netherlands, and other European states. The small size of most ACP countries means that their present importance in EC trade is relatively minimal (they account for approximately 3 per cent of EC trade).   Nonetheless, the Lome conventions include a host of provisions for industrial and technical assistance, and co-operation.   These have laid the groundwork for increased trade and investment activity as the economies of these countries evolve (Morrice 1985).

2.3. Mediterranean Countries

A series of separate agreements with a number of countries around the Mediterranean provide for various forms of industrial and other co-operation and, in many cases, allow for free access to the Community of all or some of their products, and vice-versa. These include the agreements, intended to lead to a customs union, with Cyprus, Malta, and Turkey, and the free-access agreements with seven Arab nations in Northern Africa and the Middle East.

2.4. Eastern Europe

While there are no comprehensive trade agreements between the EC and Eastern European countries, both tradition and proximity, as well as some bilateral agreements between individual countries, result in substantial trade flows in both directions between the two (a good discussion of co-operative efforts between the EC and the Council for Mutual Economic Assistance [CMEA] can be found in Feld 1984).   West German exports to Eastern Europe are about double those of the U.S., and total EC exports are twice as high as those of the U.S., Japan, and Canada combined (Conference Board 1980; see also Table IX, above).

2.5. Implications of External EC Agreements

The significance of these trade agreements (or of custom and geography, in the case of Eastern Europe) to Canada and other non-EC countries stems from their three potential implications. First, preferential access to certain markets is possible only for companies that possess an EC operational base. Second, EC-based firms can import several types of resource materials free of duty (most notably from the many resource-rich ACP states). Finally, the presence of preferential trade arrangements between the EC and a given partner can result in substantial trade losses to third countries. The United Kingdom, whose deteriorating trade with Canada has already been noted in the Introduction, is a case in point. Because of their special importance for Canada, these agreements will be discussed in more detail later in this essay.

3.   A Comment on the Present and Future Status of the EC

Several economists, political scientists and integration experts around the world tend to regard the "European unification" experiment as a failure. Critics of the Community point to extraordinary delays in decision-making, the slow (if any) progress toward political unification, the well-publicized internal EC disagreements over the Community budget and other similar facts, as examples that it has failed to reach its objectives and may soon disintegrate. Such opinions are rather strongly held; some Canadian business and government representatives stated that, at least for trade purposes, they prefer to see the countries of Western Europe as independent entities and disregard the presence of the EC if at all possible.

To what extent are such views valid? The question is difficult to answer and has been the subject of extensive discussion. Nonetheless, an overview of the present status and potential future role of the EC can serve as a useful background to the next two chapters. The following points outline some of the key dimensions in EC affairs today and suggest possible developments that may occur over the foreseeable future. This discussion does not examine purely internal Community issues (e.g. internal politics, the budget or the competition policy), or well-known facts (e.g. the slow rate of growth of most West European economies), which lie beyond the scope of this essay. Rather, it focuses on those questions that are felt to be germane to developing a long-term perspective on the EC, especially from the standpoint of the third-party (in this case Canadian) exporter or investor.

3.1. Internal Market

Perhaps the most important objective of the Treaty of Rome was the creation of a truly integrated internal market. Progress in this area has been slow but certainly not insignificant. The perceptions about, and conduct toward, the EC on the part of third-country firms can have a substantial impact on their ability to compete effectively inside the Community. This is so because of three principal factors:

a.   In the 27 years since its inception the EC has managed to almost totally eliminate internal tariff barriers[2] and to reduce non-tariff barriers by an appreciable extent, concerning merchandise trade. More importantly, Community law has been quite effective in protecting the rights of establishment and of sale, which prevent member states from discriminating against firms or products from other members. Thus although the complete harmonization of intra-Community law has not yet come about, member states do treat other-EC firms as their own in most sectors. As many European and Canadian business people pointed out in this study, it is frequently more difficult to conduct business across provincial or state boundaries in Canada or the U.S., than across the borders of EC member nations.

b.   As a corollary to the development of an integrated internal market, the Community established at the outset a common "external tariff wall". This was a key factor in the growth of intra-EC trade. Yet the common external tariff is much less of a formidable obstacle to third-country firms than it is often made to be. In fact, this tariff "wall" is not much unlike the case of Canada's FIRA, which was discussed earlier, since the importance of both as effective barriers was largely perceptual and over-rated. Some exceptions do, of course, exist. One of the most notable cases is agriculture, which is discussed below. Overall, however, the Community's external tariffs are generally similar to, and in some cases lower than, those of the U.S., Japan, and Canada (see also Ch. IV.1).

c.   External non-tariff barriers are not much different in the EC than in other DMEs. As discussed in a variety of studies (e.g. Salehizadeh 1983) these are similar to, and often less extensive than, those in countries ranging from Japan to Brazil – and, in some cases, Canada.

3.2. The Common Agricultural Policy

At its inception, the Community established a number of broad and far-reaching common economic policies. None of these has created as many problems for the EC and many of its trade partners as the Common Agricultural Policy (CAP). Because of its special importance for Canada, this will be discussed briefly here (see also Stone 1984 for a discussion of the CAP especially in relation to the GATT and to Canada).

Agriculture is particularly significant for the EC. It accounts for about 8 per cent of its labour force (Canada: 5.5 per cent; the source for these and the following statistics is Basic Statistics of the Community, EUROSTAT 1984). In some countries, the proportion is considerably higher (e.g. Greece 30 per cent, Spain and Portugal about 20 per cent, Ireland 17 per cent). In light of this, the principal aims of the CAP were to secure farmers' incomes, to achieve self-sufficiency and to harmonize national policies in agriculture. The CAP's successes have also been the cause of its problems. On the one hand, the policy succeeded in making the EC the largest food producer in the world and in reducing substantially its reliance on food imports. On the other hand, its farm subsidy programs helped generate massive surpluses in many agricultural sectors.

The EC's ratios of self-sufficiency in most agricultural and related sectors help portray the magnitude of the problem. For instance, these ratios stand at 154 per cent for sugar, 128 per cent for butter, and 119 per cent for wheat. The ratios are even higher on a country-by-country basis. In the case of butter, the degree of self-sufficiency is 233 per cent in Denmark, 298 per cent in Ireland, and no less than 467 per cent in the Netherlands. Similarly, the ratio for rice in Italy is 249 per cent; for sugar in Belgium, 293 per cent; for pork in Denmark, 395 per cent; and for veal in the Netherlands, 714 per cent.

In view of this, it is not surprising that the CAP has been the cause of friction both within the Community and in terms of its relations with its major trade partners. Internally, the policy created both budgeting and political problems. Having established a benchmark of expectations for subsidies, the EC subsequently found that it was almost impossible to adjust the CAP in the face of opposition by powerful sectoral and national lobbies.

Concerning external trade, the CAP generated a three-fold problem. The first stems from its trigger-price mechanisms which impose an automatic surcharge on many imported products, thus reducing the price-competitiveness of foreign goods in the EC. Second, the subsidy program improves the competitiveness of Community exports in third markets and often results in preempting the exports of other competitors such as Canada, the U.S., or Australia. Finally, the very presence of the CAP, coupled with the enormous problems it helped create, attracted a disproportionately large amount of attention and thus resulted in reducing the relative importance of progress made by the Community in other sectors.

It should be noted that, following several years of negotiations, the Community's members appear to have reached a preliminary understanding aimed at re-structuring the CAP. This is described in a Green Paper published by the European Commission in July 1985. It is not yet clear whether this will result in concrete measures that will help resolve the CAP's problems internally, not to mention those concerning external trade. Nonetheless, this agreement appears to be a first step in the right direction. Until it is finalized, however, it appears safe to assume that exporting certain agricultural products to the EC will remain difficult. Canada's interests in this matter, in view of the fact that its potential exports are often in areas where the CAP has created an over-capacity in the EC, will be highlighted later in this essay (see Ch. III.3).

3.3.   Political and Monetary Co-operation
The development of an integrated internal market was seen from the beginning as an "engine" that could lead to the lessening of rivalries among the Community's members and the enhancement of their roles in the global environment. These aims were in fact explicitly stated in the 1958 Treaty of Rome. In the aftermath of World War II, these were considered by some as the first steps towards complete political unification in Western Europe. With hindsight, however, a "United States of Europe" does not seem to be a plausible concept for the foreseeable future.

Progress in the political sphere has been slow, and powerful national interests often result in substantial friction within the EC. Nonetheless, some advances have been made. These include the agreement on a common European passport, which is already being issued to citizens of the member nations across the Community; the fact that the EC is represented separately, and in addition to its individual members, in various countries (e.g. Canada, the U.S., Australia) and international institutions (e.g. the GATT and the U.N.); and the "one voice" policy that has been implemented on a variety of foreign affairs issues, ranging from the Conference on Security and Co-operation in Europe to the EC stance on the Afghanistan crisis.

More important than the above steps, however, especially from the viewpoint of Canada or any third country interested in trade and investment with the EC, are two additional issues which should be mentioned here. The first refers to the political stability that the Community has brought about. The accession of socialist governments in several member states (e.g. France, Italy, Greece, Spain), along with the presence of conservative governments elsewhere (e.g. in Great Britain and West Germany), have helped demonstrate that co-operation is possible in spite of political differences, and that membership in the EC can serve as a stabilizing factor in the internal national politics of individual members. Both of these can be important factors for foreign exporters and investors, to whom political stability is a partial prerequisite for the undertaking of international economic activity.

The second issue refers to monetary co-operation within the EC. In terms of its purely economic and financial implications, discussion of this issue lies beyond the scope of this essay. It is mentioned here because several researchers feel that monetary union is a necessary pre-condition to increased political co-operation. This was, for instance, the theme of a speech entitled "A Common Currency for Europe: Now?", given by Dr. Antonio Martino of the University of Rome at a Conference Board of Canada – Department of External Affairs presentation in May 1985. As in other areas, advances in this regard have been slow. Some recent developments suggest, however, that progress is possible. These include the European Monetary System, established in 1979, the European Monetary Co-operation Fund and the rising importance of Eurobonds, which were recently floated on the New York Stock Exchange for the first time.

It is interesting that a recent poll in Europe ("Europeans and the ECU" 1985) also found strong public support for a common currency. Of those surveyed, 59 per cent indicated they support the concept of a "parallel" European currency, co-existing with national currencies, and a surprising 32 per cent supported the concept of a common currency actually replacing national currencies (those not supporting these concepts were 18 per cent and 38 per cent respectively).

From the point of view of the external observer, these developments and views signify the presence of the will (both among Europe's political leaders and within the public at large) to continue strengthening the Community's role in the future.

3.4. *Public Support for the EC*

Despite the many problems of the Community, the citizens of its member countries have shown a surprising resilience in their support for the unification objective. To the extent that political and economic events are ultimately shaped by the opinions of individual citizens, as these are expressed in aggregate public opinion, this indicates that, regardless of its slow growth, the EC is likely to survive and progress. Table XIV provides a summary of key views concerning the Community, based on public opinion polls conducted by EUROSTAT between 1971-1984. The figures in that table portray vividly the extent of public support for the EC.

3.5. Exaggerated expectations

More often than not the EC is judged against exaggerated expectations rather than against pragmatic reality. The post-World War II euphoria created understandable expectations for an early and complete European union. The task, however, was not easy. It involved bringing together 10 (now 12) countries, representing 270 million people, who speak seven different languages, and who had been at war against each other for most of their 2,500-year history. The enormity of this task escaped the attention of most observers in the EC's early years and is largely disregarded by its critics as late as today. Yet when one compares that situation to, for instance, Canada's difficulty in repatriating its constitution under much more favourable conditions, one cannot help but ask, as Diebold did in 1968: "... the European Community has not created a United States of Europe or even a full economic union – but who has a right to expect that?"

3.6. Direction vs. speed of progress

As is evident from the preceding points, most of the criticism directed at the EC is grounded on the fact that the Community has not moved fast enough, rather than because of disagreement with the direction it is taking. Comments made recently by several opinion-leading industrialists in Europe indicate both disenchantment with growth to-date and a desire to see a more closely integrated Europe. For instance (Kransdorff 1984):

> The EC should "push on with integration, create that whole market at last which we have been waiting for ..." (K.H. Berlet, a director of West Germany's Hoechst).

> "The banks play an essentially supportive role in Europe's progress towards full integration. But that progress would undoubtedly quicken if the barriers to free trade in financial services were lowered" (C. Green, a director of National Westminster Bank, U.K.).

TABLE XIV. Attitudes of EC Citizens toward the Community

Issue	Time of Survey													
	07/71	09/73	11/76	11/77	11/78	1975-1982 (average)	04/80	10/80	10/81	10/82	04/83	10/83	04/84	10/84
1. "Next year will be better" (% agreeing)								20	25	25			26	29
2. "World war probable in next 10 years" (% agreeing)				14					24	18			19	13
3. "Joint action better for security and defence" (% agreeing)	12			48	50		34				65			64
4. Overall attitude – "Community a good thing" (index 3-1)		2.52				2.46					2.43	2.47	2.48	2.49
5. "My country has benefitted from EC membership" (% agreeing)											52		46	48
6. "My country has benefitted more than others from EC membership" (index 3-1)														
7. Support for West European unification (index 4-1)											1.84	1.84		1.83
8. Attitude toward idea of "United States of Europe" (index 3-1)		3.19				3.15					3.21		3.10	3.19
9. "European unification should be speeded up" (index 3-1)														2.34
Opinion Leaders + +		2.66												2.53
+ +		2.48												2.46
Non-Leaders -		2.29												2.36
- -		2.16												2.25

Source: Commission of the European Communities, EUROBAROMETER, No. 22 December 1984
Note: The index indicators, in parentheses above, show the index's highest and lowest value; the highest value corresponds to agreement with the statement in question.

In conclusion, it may be said that progress in the EC has been and will continue to be slow. There appears to be no doubt, however, as to the Community's continuing and growing role in global economic and political affairs. Perhaps the most relevant comment concerning the future of the Community was that made by Ball (1976:125): "Pan-European enthusiasm could revive rapidly if actual dismantling of the European Community appeared imminent".

Notes

1. The European Community (or "Communities", as it is often referred to) consists of the European Economic Community, the European Coal and Steel Community, and the European Atomic Energy Community. It now consists of 12 member states and is run by five major institutions. The Commission, with 16 members, is the EC's main initiator and executor of policy and decisions. The Council of Ministers, with 12 members, is the main decision-making body. The directly elected Parliament, with 518 members, oversees the Commission and the Council, has the power to dismiss the Commission by a two-thirds majority, and is principally involved with the Community's budget. The Court of Justice, with 13 judges, adjudicates EC law and is empowered to hear cases submitted by any one of the governments, corporations, individuals, or other institutions of the EC. Finally, the Economic and Social Committee, with 189 members split into several subcommittees, advises other EC institutions on policy.

    The unique and little understood characteristics of the institutions that form the EC is that they represent an effective system of checks and balances for any EC activity. Although this is often a main reason behind delays in decision-making, it also helps reduce friction among special interest groups and it ensures that, once approved, EC decisions are likely to be quickly and easily implemented. The system owes its uniqueness to the various interests that each institution represents. Specifically, the Commission's role is to protect and enhance Community interests; the Council represents the national interests of the member-states; the Parliament sits by political party rather than by nationality, and therefore represents all of the EC's political hues; the Court is open to cases brought by any individual, group, or government inside the EC; finally, the Economic and Social Committee sits by major interest group (business, labour, government, and consumer). Thus all possible EC matters are inextricably linked from every possible angle, and each individual or group is represented at the EC level in one way or another.

In addition to the sources listed in the References section of this essay, more information on the basic characteristics of the EC can be found in a variety of publications which are easily available through the Community's delegations in Canada, the U.S., and many other countries. In Canada, the Journal of European Integration is exclusively devoted to discussions and analyses of issues related to the EC and the more general subject of integration.

2. While internal tariffs among the EC's original members have been eliminated, some tariffs still remain in the Community — especially in the cases of Greece, Spain and Portugal. The intent in retaining them is to ease the integration of these newer entrants into the overall EC economy. These barriers are being phased out gradually, based on timetables that are often tied to the rate of improvement of the economies of the new members.

Chapter III:

Trade and Investment Between Canada and the EC

> "Our market share in Europe has declined in the
> last 25 years .... There was an improvement in
> 1984; it remains a priority objective to
> enlarge our market share, particularly for
> manufactured goods".
>
> *The Right Hon. Joe Clark*
> *Secretary of State for External Affairs*
> *Competitiveness and Security; Ottawa 1985*

The two previous chapters outlined the international trade and
investment performance of Canada and the EC. Each chapter
examined one of the two trade partners separately, but not in
isolation from, the other. The purpose was to focus on those
elements of Canada's and the EC's international economic
activity that directly affect the relationship between the two and
that are therefore relevant to the discussion that follows. Several
comparative statistics and trends were examined between the
Community and Canada, and between these two entities and
other major actors in the international arena, such as the U.S.
and Japan. The purpose of this chapter is to discuss, in
considerably more detail, the trade and investment flows both
eastward and westward across the Atlantic. This chapter
consists of three main parts: the first reviews trade flows, the
second is a brief examination of investment patterns, and the
third analyzes the factors that gave rise to the present state of
affairs between the two partners.

1.   Recent Trends and Present Status in Canada-EC Trade

Tables XV to XIX inclusive provide a comprehensive and
analytical image of trade between Canada and the Community.
A number of interesting observations can be made from these
tables. These are summarized below.

1.1. Trends in Canadian Imports from the EC

Community products declined steadily in relative importance to Canada between 1968 and 1980, but this trend was arrested and actually reversed slightly between 1980-1984. Using 1978 as a base year, the growth of total Canadian imports outpaced that of imports from the EC during the entire 1978-1984 period. However, using the immediately preceding period for reference, the reverse occurred after 1980, with Canada's imports from the EC rising slightly faster than total imports and reaching an 8.6 per cent share of the total by 1984 (Table XV). In relative terms, imports into Canada rose faster on the part of four of the smallest EC nations: Belgium, Luxembourg, Denmark and the Netherlands.

1.2. Trends in Canadian Exports to the EC

The relative importance of the Community as an export destination for Canada declined rapidly and steadily between 1968-1984 (Table XVI). With the exception of a significant but temporary increase between 1978-1980, which brought EC's share in Canadian exports to 12.8 per cent, Canadian exports to other countries (most notably to the U.S.; see also Tables I and III) rose faster than those to the EC.

This holds true regardless of whether 1978 or the immediately preceding period is used as a reference point. As a result of this decline, the EC's share in Canada's exports reached an all-time low of 6.4 per cent in 1984, down from 9 per cent in 1982. It must be noted, however, that this decline reflects more the rapid rise in total Canadian exports (33 per cent between 1982-1984) than a significant decrease in Canada's exports to the EC in value terms. Exports to individual EC countries remained relatively stable over these three years, while the total declined marginally from $7.6 billion to $7.2 billion (this decline is, of course, steeper in volume terms).

1.3. Canada's Trade Balance with the EC

Canada has posted an overall trade surplus every year since 1968, with the exception of 1975. The same favourable record had characterized this country's performance in relation to the European Community until 1983. Following that year, the stability in exports to the EC, coupled with the increase in imports from it, combined to produce for the first time a deficit of slightly over $1 billion for Canada. As Table XVII indicates, this trend is particularly important to Canada in light of the traditional contribution of EC trade to this country's usual

TABLE XV. Canadian Imports from the EC
(million Canadian $)

Exporting Country	1984	1982	1980	1978	1972	1968
United Kingdom	2,319	1,904	1,974	1,609	950	696
Ireland	187	129	101	57	17	10
Belgium + Lux.	447	264	251	208	90	58
Denmark	201	129	120	97	48	26
France	1,219	877	773	680	251	122
West Germany	2,174	1,384	1,455	1,254	513	299
Greece	41	30	31	36	NA	NA
Italy	1,116	725	611	520	204	115
Netherlands	545	267	264	227	92	69
Total Canadian Imports from EC-10	8,249	5,709	5,580	4,688	2,165	1,395
Total Canadian Imports	95,842	67,856	69,128	50,108	18,669	12,360
Imports from EC-10 as % of Total Canadian Imports	8.6	8.4	8.1	9.4	11.6	11.3
Growth in Imports 1978 = 100						
a. from EC-10	176	122	119	100	46	30
b. total	191	135	138	100	37	25
prev.period = 100 (e.g. 1984/1982, 1982/1980)						
a. from EC-10	144	102	119	217	155	100
b. total	141	98	138	268	151	100

Source: Statistics Canada, Imports-Merchandise Trade (annual, Cat.65-203) and Review of Foreign Trade 1966-1972 (occasional, Cat.65-501)

TABLE XVI. Canadian Exports to the EC
(million Canadian $)

Importing Country	1984	1982	1980	1978	1972	1968
United Kingdom	2,540	2,727	3,245	2,007	1,343	1,210
Ireland	99	99	116	31	15	11
Belgium + Lux.	696	791	1,002	486	197	127
Denmark	99	87	89	64	18	16
France	732	755	1,017	478	154	82
West Germany	1,255	1,285	1,668	792	313	229
Greece	50	77	130	57	24	9
Italy	598	705	1,004	486	201	131
Netherlands	1,088	1,060	1,442	574	252	179
Total Canadian Exports to EC-10	7,157	7,586	9,713	4,975	2,517	1,994
Total Canadian Exports	112,495	84,530	76,159	52,842	20,064	13,680
Exports to EC-10 as % of Total Canadian Exports	6.4	9.0	12.8	9.4	12.5	14.6
Growth in Exports 1978 = 100						
a. to EC-10	144	152	195	100	51	40
b. total	213	160	144	100	38	26
prev.period = 100 (e.g. 1984/1982, 1982/1980)						
a. to EC-10	94	78	195	198	126	100
b. total	133	111	144	263	147	100

Source: Statistics Canada, Exports-Merchandise Trade
(annual, Cat.65-202) and Review of Foreign Trade
1966-1972 (occasional, Cat.65-501)

**TABLE XVII. Canadian Balance of Merchandise Trade
with the EC
(million Canadian $)**

	1984	1982	1980	1978	1972	1968
Exports to EC	7,157	7,586	9,713	4,975	2,517	1,994
Imports from EC	8,249	5,709	5,580	4,688	2,165	1,395
Balance of Trade for Canada with the EC	(1,092)	1,877	4,133	287	352	599
Total Canadian Exports	112,495	84,530	76,159	52,842	20,064	13,680
Total Canadian Imports	95,842	67,856	69,128	50,108	18,669	12,360
Balance of Trade for Canada – Total	16,653	16,674	7,031	2,734	1,395	1,320
Balance of Trade with the EC as % of Total Canadian Balance of Trade	(6.6)	11.3	58.8	10.5	25.2	45.4

Source: Tables XV and XVI.

balance of trade position: between 1968 and 1983, this contribution ranged from 11 per cent to 59 per cent of Canada's total
merchandise trade surplus.

1.4. Composition of Canada-EC trade
1.4.1 Overview

Chapter I addressed in some detail Canada's weakness in
manufactured exports and, more generally, in manufacturing as
a whole. This weakness is equally apparent specifically in its
relationship with the EC, although some improvement has
occurred over the past few years. Table XVIII shows that the vast
majority of imports from the EC consists of end products and
fabricated materials[1] (50.8 per cent and 29.1 per cent in 1984,
respectively), both of which contain a high degree of processing.
Nonetheless, this high proportion of manufactured imports
represents a decline from the respective statistics of 1978,
especially in end products.

On the export side, as shown in the same table, Canada's
strength in relation to the EC is concentrated in fabricated and
crude materials[2] (41.9 per cent and 27 per cent respectively in
1984). These statistics represent a proportionate decline in
fabricated materials from 45.3 per cent of the total in 1978, which
was accompanied by a concurrent rise in the proportion of crude
materials (from 22.7 per cent in 1978) and of end products (from
11.6 per cent in 1978 to 15.2 per cent in 1984). On aggregate,
therefore, the exports of manufactured products remained stable
in the period under study: fabricated materials along with end
products accounted for 56.9 per cent of the total in 1978, and for
57.1 per cent in 1984. The relative increase in the proportion of
crude materials in Canada's exports to the EC is thus explained
by the roughly equivalent decline in the value of the Food,
Beverages and Tobacco sector from 18.5 per cent in 1978 to 12.4
per cent in 1984 (Table XVIII).

Table XIX provides some further detail on Canada's end-
product exports to the EC. These exports increased steadily
between 1978-1980 in proportion to total exports to the Community, but then stabilized at around 15 per cent between 1980-
1984.

1.4.2. Agriculture and Fisheries

Because agriculture and fisheries represent a significant
component of Canadian exports, they warrant a brief but
separate mention here. Concerning agriculture, it was
mentioned earlier that the Common Agricultural Policy resulted
in massive surpluses within the EC in several areas. The effect of

TABLE XVIII. Composition of Canada-EC Trade

	Live animals	Food, feed beverages, tobacco	Crude materials, inedible	Fabricated materials, inedible	End products, inedible	Re-exports and/or Special Transactions	Total Exports
			1. Exports to EC-10				
Value (million Canadian $)							
1984	12	885	1,930	3,000	1,089	240	7,157
1978	7	922	1,130	2,254	577	85	4,975
Distribution (%)							
1984	0.2	12.4	27.0	41.9	15.2	3.4	100
1978	0.1	18.5	22.7	45.3	11.6	1.7	100
			2. Imports from EC-10				
Value (million Canadian $)							
1984	2	838	655	2,402	4,194	158	8,249
1978	1	497	97	1,257	2,772	64	4,688
Distribution (%)							
1984	0	10.2	7.9	29.1	50.8	1.9	100
1978	0	10.6	2.1	26.8	59.1	1.4	100

Source: Statistics Canada, Imports-Merchandise Trade and Exports-Merchandise Trade (annuals, Cat. 65-203 and 65-202).

**TABLE XIX. Canadian End-Product Exports to EC
(percentage distribution)**

Importing Country	1984	1982	1980	1979	1978
United Kingdom	15	15	12	11	11
Ireland	65	70	47	46	45
Belgium + Luxembourg	8	9	9	10	10
Denmark	19	29	24	18	19
France	19	18	13	16	15
West Germany	15	16	26	24	15
Greece	18	25	17	24	25
Italy	14	14	8	7	7
Netherlands	14	10	11	7	8
EC-10	15	15	14	13	11

Source: Statistics Canada, Exports-Merchandise Trade (annual, Cat. 65-202)

these surpluses has been increased competition between the Community and other agricultural exporters in third markets, and reduced access to the EC itself by external producers.

For Canada, the impact of the CAP has been particularly severe because of its traditional strength in agricultural exports. Nadeau (1985) has discussed this impact at length, especially in relation to the effect of Great Britain's membership in the EC. In summary, he shows that with the exception of meat products and animal feeds,Canadian exports to Great Britain declined drastically in most other agricultural sub-sectors such as wheat, barley, oilseeds, tobacco and cheese. The following data provide a more general overview of the declining contribution of agriculture in Canada's exports to the EC.

	Selected Years				
Exports to EC	*1966*	*1970*	*1975*	*1980*	*1984*
Total (million $)	1,774	2,610	4,095	9,272	6,981
Agriculture (million $)	407	401	704	886	782
Agriculture as % of total	23	15	17	10	11
Fisheries (million $)	2	5	11	63	40
Fisheries as % of total	0.1	0.2	0.3	0.7	0.6

(Note: All dollar amounts are in current dollars.
Source: Commodity Trade 1985)

As is evident from this table, agricultural products now account for about half of their earlier strength as a proportion of total Canadian exports to the EC.

Concerning fisheries, Canada was able to conclude a long-term agreement on fisheries with the EC. The above data suggest the positive effect of the agreement. Unlike agriculture, the contribution of fish products to total Canadian exports to the EC grew and remained steady (though comparatively small) in the periods preceding and following the signing of the agreement in 1981. This agreement was made possible due, in large part, to Canada's rich fish stocks off the Atlantic coast, which provided a negotiating tool that could be used in exchange for improved access to the European market. As Barry (1985) put it,

> "the cornerstone of the agreement was an exchange of concessions that gave Canada improved terms of access to the EC market for certain fish products in return for Community fishing rights for certain species inside Canada's 200-mile Atlantic offshore zone" (p. 6).

Barry's thorough discussion of the background to this agreement, and future expectations from it, makes it unnecessary to elaborate on this subject. It is interesting to note, however, a main point that permeates his tracing of the four-year-long negotiations that led to the conclusion of this six-year agreement in 1981. The author shows that much of the difficulty surrounding its development and implementation was the result of internal political concerns on each side of the Atlantic. These concerns reflect the variety of provincial interests within Canada and of national interests within the EC. For instance, these included Newfoundland's attempt to tie the fisheries agreement to the EC's intention, put into effect later, to ban seal skin imports, and Great Britain's attempt to place a ceiling on imports from Canada in order to protect its market from being flooded by cheaper Canadian fish products. From the vantage point of this essay, this variety of regional interests lends support to a point made earlier: that the importance of intra-EC variations is often over-rated, since similar variations are often found in federal political systems as well, including those of Canada and the U.S.

2.   Canada-EC Foreign Direct Investment

The statistical note (No. 5) in the Introduction made reference to the relative paucity and dated nature of statistics on foreign direct investment flows and stocks. Yet some recent figures have lately become available concerning FDI stocks by Canada in other countries and by foreign investors in Canada. These show that FDI patterns between Canada and the EC are not much different from the trade patterns that were examined earlier. The relevant statistics are shown in Tables XX and XXI.

The first of these tables includes the stock of Canadian FDI in the Community, the U.S. and the rest of the world. The relevant statistics are given both in value terms and in percentage distribution. The Community's share in CFDI remained relatively stable at about 15-17 per cent until 1980. During the same period, the United States' share increased steadily from 52 per cent to 64 per cent of CFDI, while the share of all other countries declined from 32 per cent to 22 per cent. These trends changed starting in 1981. By 1984, the Community's share had dropped to 8 per cent of the total and that of the U.S. to 57 per cent, while that of all other countries rose to beyond its earlier strength and reached 34 per cent.

Similarly, as in the case of imports into Canada, the origins of inward FDI has remained remarkably stable at approximately 16 per cent for the EC, 79 per cent for the United States, and 5 per cent with respect to all other origins over the recent past.

It is important to note that these statistics are based on the book value of FDI at the end of each of the years given. They are thus sensitive to the accounting procedures concerning currency valuation and recording rates that are used by the reporting firms. Because of the recent appreciation of the Canadian dollar in relation to European currencies and its devaluation compared to the U.S. dollar, it is likely that assets in Europe are under-

TABLE XX. Foreign Direct Investment by and in Canada

Year		Locations or Origins						
	EC	U.S.	Other	Total	EC	U.S.	Other	Total

1. Stock of FDI by Canada

Year	EC	U.S.	Other	Total	EC	U.S.	Other	Total
	(cum. book value-billion C$)				(percentage distribution)			
1975	1.6	5.5	3.4	10.5	15	52	32	100
1976	1.7	6.1	3.7	11.5	15	53	32	100
1977	2.3	7.1	4.1	13.5	17	53	30	100
1978	2.5	9.0	4.9	16.4	15	55	30	100
1979	3.3	12.1	4.6	20.0	17	61	23	100
1980	3.8	16.4	5.6	25.8	15	64	22	100
1981	4.0	19.9	8.6	32.5	15	61	26	100
1982	3.4	19.6	10.9	33.9	12	58	32	100
1983	3.0	21.2	11.7	35.9	10	59	33	100
1984	3.4	23.8	14.2	41.4	8	57	34	100

2. Stock of FDI in Canada

Year	EC	U.S.	Other	Total	EC	U.S.	Other	Total
	(cum. book value-billion C$)				(percentage distribution)			
1975	5.8	29.7	1.9	37.4	16	79	5	100
1976	6.5	31.9	1.9	40.3	16	79	5	100
1977	6.9	34.7	2.1	43.7	16	79	5	100
1978	7.5	38.3	2.5	48.3	16	79	5	100
1979	8.7	42.8	2.8	54.3	16	79	5	100
1980	9.6	48.7	3.3	61.6	16	79	5	100

Sources: Statistics Canada, Canada's International Investment Position (annual, Cat.67-202). Deeg 1985.

represented, while those in the U.S. are over-represented, when expressed in Canadian dollars. The reverse is true for foreign-origin investments in Canada (Deeg 1985).

Another factor that must be borne in mind when examining Canadian-EC FDI statistics is the effect of the flurry of acquisitions of foreign-controlled firms in Canada by domestic enterprises (e.g. the purchase of Fina by Petro-Canada). The size of some of these transactions is rather large. As a result, they have affected both the book value of foreign investment in Canada and the value of net capital flows, since large sums of capital have left the country and thus masked the value of inward investment flows.

Finally, Table XXI shows a comparative distribution of Canadian FDI in the U.S. and the U.K. among eight main industrial sectors. It will be noticed that this distribution is roughly similar for both countries as well as between them and total Canadian FDI, with three main exceptions: the strong proportions of investment in real estate in the U.S., in mining in all other countries, and in manufacturing as well as petroleum and natural gas in the U.K.

3.   Factors Affecting Canadian-EC Trade and Investment Flows

The factors that lie behind the decline in the relative importance of Canada and the European Community as trade partners are many and closely related to each other. Taken together, they provide a comprehensive background to the deterioration of a once-thriving relationship, against which future policy issues can be considered. Some of these factors are unique to the Canada-EC relationship while others are common to Canada's overall international performance (as discussed in Chapter I). The first will be examined here in more detail; for the second type, discussion will be limited to establishing their relevance to the Canada-EC relationship.

3.1. Specific Canada-EC Issues

The 1976 Framework Agreement resulted essentially in establishing a vague framework for co-operation in the economic field (see also the brief discussion in Chapter I). It was intended to provide the impetus for the formation of joint ventures between Canadian and European firms, for technological and scientific co-operation and, eventually, for an increase in inbound and outbound trade and investment flows. Few, if any, researchers or

TABLE XXI. Canadian-controlled Foreign Investment[1]

Industry	Location of Investment (percentage distribution – 1982)			
	U.S.	U.K.	Other	Total
Manufacturing	33	49	45	37
Petroleum and Natural Gas	17	22	11	16
Mining	4	0	17	7
Utilities	3	2	11	5
Merchandising	4	4	5	4
Real Estate	27	10	1	19
Other financial	8	8	8	8
Misc. other	5	6	2	4
All industries	100	100	100	100

Note: (1) "Canadian-controlled" investment consists of direct (owned by the investor or a related party) investment and of third-party (from non-related sources, emanating from other countries or from Canada) investment.

Source: Statistics Canada, The Daily, 16-04-1985, page 2.

other commentators seem to have any doubt that the agreement has failed.

Co-operation has largely taken the form of trade missions between Canada and the EC, and both entities have permanent delegations at each other's seat (Ottawa and Brussels). Yet there is every reason to believe that such activities would have occurred even if the agreement had never existed. Further, these are not unique to Canada's relations with the Community. Bilateral trade missions are commonplace among trading nations and, as already pointed out, several other countries maintain or are host to permanent delegations at or from the EC (e.g. Australia, U.S.). On the other hand, the two areas where improvements would normally have been expected – trade and investment flows – have steadily deteriorated or remained stable over the past decade, with the exception of a brief upswing around 1979-1980 (see Tables XVI and XX above).

The reasons behind the failure of the Framework Agreement are many but can be summarized in three main categories. The first two are the lack of political will to implement it and the more general failure of the "Third Option" policy which gave the agreements its original momentum, both of which were mentioned earlier. The third reason reflects the combined effect of a number of controllable and uncontrollable forces, all of which had a negative impact on Canadian-EC economic links. These are highlighted below.

3.1.1. Bilateral Irritants

The Canada-EC relationship has often been marred by unfortunate incidents arising from the policies of one or both of the two trade partners. Although diplomatic language uses the term "irritants" to describe them, they have received such widespread publicity that their impact on corporate and public decision making can be assumed to be substantial. From the Canadian side, some of the better known cases include:

a.   The problems related to Canadian cheddar cheese exports to the EC (the saga has been analyzed by Cohn 1978; see also Nadeau 1985);

b.   The last-minute quota imposed upon a shipment of pork from Canada in 1981. This was triggered by a complaint from a European pork producer to EC's Commission under the provisions of the Common Agricultural Policy. The shipment was caught in mid-ocean and neither the EC nor Canada would allow its import or re-import, respectively — the first because of the quota, the second because the product, originally destined for the EC, did not meet Canadian health standards!

c.   Violations of Canada's fishery laws and limitations — a subject that is expected to become a more important issue now that the large Spanish and Portuguese fleets have come under the aegis of the EC (see also Section 1.4.2. above);

d.   The European Community ban on seal skin imports. This was originally imposed for a two-year period starting in 1983, but has been subsequently extended to 1989 (EC News 1985); and,

e.   The lowering of the European quota on Canadian newsprint imports in 1984, following the finalization of the EC-EFTA agreement which came into full effect in 1984 and granted preferrential access to Nordic newsprint producers (see also Ch. II.2.1 and Ch. IV.1.2);

The complaints from the European side are equally numerous and have received equally large amounts of publicity in Europe as well as in Canada. Some of these are:

a. The apparent European frustration with the unwillingness of Canadian companies to buy EC products in certain sensitive areas. An example is Europe's cherished passenger plane, the Airbus, which is built by the Airbus Industrie consortium and is now the second-best selling aircraft series world-wide after Boeing[3];

b. Earlier perceptions about FIRA as an effective barrier to EC investments in Canada (as discussed above, Ch. I).

c. Perceptions about Canada's low domestic oil prices which, along with the National Energy Program, were often seen as indirect but significant subsidies to Canadian industry. It is still too early to assess the potential impact of the abolition of FIRA and the NEP on overseas investors. Both, however, have been acknowledged to be significant steps in the right direction (for example, von Franque 1986);

d. The effect on energy-hungry Europe of the Canadian ban on uranium sales following the 1977 atomic bomb tests by India; and,

e. The effect on European producers, such as the Italian leather industry, of Canada's quota protection of several sectors, including footwear and meat products.

It should be noted that these irritants are not purely inter-governmental matters which stay outside the domain of business interests except for the attention of firms that are directly affected by them. Instead, many of the business people who were interviewed for this study both in Canada and in Europe pointed out that the publicity which usually surrounds such issues tends to become internalized by business leaders and influences decision-making. This problem is further aggravated by publicity on purely domestic matters (e.g. reporting on EC's budget troubles in Canada and on Canada's constitutional debate in Europe).

3.1.2. Sectoral Complementarity and Competition

Related to the above is the issue of the similarities and differences in both strengths and weaknesses among the EC and Canada. The negative effect of many of these on the relationship between the two trading partners is manifested clearly in at least three cases:

a. Agriculture: both partners are strong in this area and depend on it for a large part of their exports. As noted, the protective measures of the CAP have resulted in a loss of exports for Canada. The fact that Canada also employs protective measures (e.g. Stone 1984:161), with similar negative effects on foreign producers does not, of course, help matters much.

b. Resources vs. Manufacturing: Canada is strong in the first, the EC in the second. This results in a lop-sided trade composition which is unfavourable to Canada, since it exports more resources to, and imports more end products from, the EC.

c. Services: Canada is particularly strong in certain service sectors. Typical examples include banking and professional services. The latter represents a particularly interesting example of competing interests. As is well known, Canada has a continuing current account deficit ($6.9 billion in 1983). Consulting and other professional services are among only a handful of sectors that are in a surplus position. This surplus reached $84 million in 1981 and reflects the international strength of Canada's consulting engineers (Jones 1985; see also Dagenais 1981). In turn, this strength is derived from the expertise of Canadian engineers in turn-key projects (e.g. in telecommunications), especially in LDCs (Wright 1981). However, the Community is also strong in this sector. This has a two-fold negative effect: first, it is difficult for Canada's consultants to penetrate European markets, because of the availability of indigenous competition; and second, engineers from both origins often have to compete fiercely against each other for projects in the Third World.

3.1.3. Currency Exchange Rates

A primary reason behind the decline in Canadian exports to the EC between 1980 and 1984, and in the stability of Canadian imports from the Community, has been the appreciation of Canada's currency against the currencies of Europe. Table XXII shows the trends in exchange rates for Canada and the EC member states between 1982 and March 1985. As can be seen, the value of the currencies of some of Canada's major trading partners fell rather substantially. For example, the French franc fell from 5.3 to 7.3 per C$, and the British pound from 0.46 to 0.64 in that period. At the same time, the Canadian dollar depreciated at a slower rate against its American counterpart, thus creating an ever-widening gulf between itself and the major European currencies.

In addition to making Canadian products more expensive for Europe, these trends have had a second negative effect for

Canada: they have made European goods cheaper than Canadian goods in the U.S. market, thus threatening this country's traditional export destination in those sectors where European and Canadian producers compete directly.

TABLE XXII. Recent Exchange Rate Fluctuations

Country	Monetary unit	National currency units per Canadian dollar			
		1982	1983	1984	1985 [1]
United States	Dollar	0.81	0.81	0.77	0.72
Belgium-Lux.	Franc	37	42	45	48
Denmark	Krone	6.7	7.4	8.0	8.5
France	Franc	5.3	6.2	6.7	7.3
West Germany	DM	2.0	2.1	2.2	2.4
Greece	Drachma	54	71	87	102
Ireland	Pound	0.57	0.65	0.71	0.77
Italy	Lira	1096	1233	1357	1505
Netherlands	Guilder	2.2	2.3	2.5	2.7
United Kingdom	Pound	0.46	0.54	0.58	0.64

Note: (1) March
Source: OECD, Main Economic Indicators, April 1985.

A representative of the Canadian Manufacturers' Association offered a recent example of this during a discussion in June 1985. This refers to the competitive strength of cement exported from Spain to North America. In spite of the transportation costs involved, its prices are so low that potential European exports of this product appear to threaten Canadian cement producers from the prairie provinces. Having entered North America via the southeastern U.S., and having been shipped northward via the Mississippi river, Spanish cement can still have a landed cost in the Toronto-Montreal markets which is much lower than that of Canadian cement.

Notwithstanding the above, it would be a mistake to attach too much importance to the role of exchange rate fluctuations in determining the direction and value of trade flows. While there is little question that an appreciating currency may affect exports adversely, this effect is more pronounced if two conditions are present: when exports tend to be opportunistic rather than long-term and strategic in character, and when they contain a strong component of undifferentiated products. Because of their relevance to Canada's international competitiveness, these two conditions warrant some more discussion here.

"Opportunistic" is used to connote exports undertaken in order to dispose of excess inventories, rather than to build a long-term presence in foreign markets. Referring to Norvell and Raveed (1980; see Note 2, Chapter I), it will be remembered that this is one of the factors that often motivate firms to consider international activity. As many of the European respondents indicated, Canadian exporters are seen in the EC as acting under exactly this type of short-term perspective (see also "Canada's Trade Challenge" 1981:25).

This finding seems to be in line with the literature on the export behaviour of the firm. It suggests rather conclusively that this type of behaviour is more likely to be found among smaller exporters (Bilkey 1978; Welch and Wiedersheim-Paul 1980). In view of this, and of the generally small size of exporting firms in Canada (as noted in Chapter I), it seems reasonably safe to assume that over-capacity and excess inventories may indeed be prime motivating factors behind a large proportion of Canadian exports. In turn, this can explain partially why, in the face of adverse currency conditions, there is a lack of buyer loyalty and of producer persistence in preserving a trade relationship, with the resultant loss of markets.

The second of the above-mentioned conditions refers to the effects of currency fluctuations on the trading of undifferentiated products. These effects are similar to those of opportunistic exports. Price plays a disproportionately major role in both cases. In the case of undifferentiated goods, the lack of distinctive features reduces the potential benefits that might arise from brand loyalty and from long-term buyer-seller relationships. As already noted, a large proportion of Canadian exports consists of agricultural, resource and intermediate commodities and products. This, then, can provide an additional explanation for the apparent ease in supplier substitution which is exemplified by Canada's declining exports to the EC over the past few years.

3.1.4. *Recovering Canadian Economy*

As was noted in Chapter I, Canadian governments have tended to shift their attention from diversification to continentalist policies, and vice-versa, depending on the overall strength of the domestic economy. Two alternate explanations were offered in that discussion concerning the reasons behind such shifts: that policy makers appear to be less concerned with diversification when the Canadian economy is strong, or when it is weak. Either way, an additional reason behind the recent decline in Canada-EC trade can, therefore, be found in the switch from recession to recovery between the late 1970s and the early 1980s: the pro-continentalist mood that seems to be prevalent today may be due either to the current economic strength or to the immediately preceding weakness.

3.1.5. *Perceived Importance of the EC*

One of the most interesting, and in a sense surprising, findings of the present study has been the apparent reluctance of Canadian decision and policy makers to acknowledge the presence and role of the EC as one entity to any significant extent at any but the diplomatic level. In many interviews and discussions with Canadian business and government officials over five years, it has become clear that most perceive the EC as a vast and unnecessary bureaucracy which can and must be disregarded whenever possible.

Most prefer to see Canada-EC issues on a country-by-country basis. Naturally, this view tends to focus more on the U.K., France and, to a lesser extent, West Germany, for any one or more of cultural, economic size, historical and other reasons. This attitude is also evident in several manifestations of government practice, such as the organizational structure of the European bureaux at federal departments, the number of economic officers assigned specifically to EC affairs, or the aggregate reporting of trade by regions on the part of Statistics Canada. In all of these instances, the EC is paid lip-service at best. For example, the EC countries are not grouped together in the trade development desks at the Department of External Affairs; Statistics Canada reports aggregate import figures for Western Europe but not for the EC, and exports separately for the U.K. and "other EC" states; and so on.

This view appears to be based on the obvious and numerous differences between the EC's member states, but is certainly not shared by non-Canadian, non-EC business people who were interviewed in the course of this study; nor is it shared by international institutions. Not only EFTA's statistical bureau but also those of the IMF, the World Bank, the OECD and various United Nations' agencies acknowledge the relative importance of the EC as a trading entity and report aggregate statistics for the Community in addition to those of its members.

In addition, American and European business people have repeatedly stated that, if at all possible, they attempt to take advantage of the abolition of tariff and reduction of non-tariff barriers inside the Community by developing EC-wide strategies and using Community-level distribution and promotion channels, product designs and pricing systems. A good example of this approach is Westinghouse. For many of its product lines, the company supplies all EC members from a central warehouse located in the Shannon free trade zone in Ireland. This allows Westinghouse to bring its products within the EC's geographic domain while at the same time deferring the payment of duties by technically keeping them "outside" the EC's external tariff wall. When demand in a given EC market warrants their release from the free zone, duties are paid and the goods are technically brought inside the Community, thus being free to be shipped to any of its members without further delay. (*Journal of Commerce* 1983; also see Anderson 1972; Cracco and Robert 1974; *Business Week* 1966; Kravis 1962).

From an applied perspective, the implication of Canadian attitudes in relation to the Community is that they result in a failure to take advantage of the opportunities that are available through the internal harmonization, incomplete as it may be, that the EC has brought about. By considering each EC country separately in the process of market assessment, Canadian decision and policy makers are thus faced with much smaller market sizes than EC-wide strategies would indicate. This attitude may also help to explain the following point, which was instrumental in Canada's inability to develop and maintain a strong presence in the Community.

3.1.6. Slow Response to EC Evolution

One of the major accomplishments for which American business people have often been credited is their foresight in perceiving the future importance of the EC while negotiations were still under way for its creation. Partially as a result of this foresight, American businesses invested heavily in Europe in the years leading to the 1958 Treaty of Rome which established the EC. They were thus able to minimize the effects of the Community's external tariff wall. As stated by McEvoy (1974):

"U.S. industry ... quickly recognized the enormous potential available through this sudden agglomeration of consumers, ... its vast resources were concentrated on establishing itself in this enormous new market, and hence the U.S.-based multinational began to take shape" (p. 669).

Further, U.S. corporations were able to foresee the potential impact of EC's agreements with other regions or countries. Upon the signing of the EC-EFTA agreement in 1971, Anderson (1972) forecasted its enormous potential for rationalization and expansion of business operations. He pointed out that firms with production operations in either the EC or EFTA would now be able to reach, free of tariffs, an expanded market of over 300 million people. At the same time, those with production operations in both the EC and EFTA would be able to reorganize and reduce their operating costs within the European free trading system. Similarly, an early study by Baker and Ryans (1972), addressed to half of the top 100 MNCs in *Fortune* magazine's "500 List", shows that many executives saw the Community as a jumping-off point for other markets. About 63 per cent of the respondents in the study reported sales increases to EC members, 25 per cent to non-EC countries, and 6 per cent to the U.S. itself, all attributed directly to the formation of the EC and their ability to operate within it.

With few exceptions, similar statements cannot be made in regard to the speed with which Canadian-owned or controlled enterprises[4] responded first to the formation of the EC and then to its enlargements and its association with EFTA, the ACP nations, and other regions and countries (see, for example, EEC Expands ... 1973). A study of a small number of Canadian firms investing in Europe states that most of them engaged in offshore FDI primarily when difficulties in exporting, coupled with a need for larger markets, forced them to do so (Abdel-Malek 1983). Notwithstanding the small sample size of the study, this finding appears to support the hypothesis that Canadian companies tend to behave reactively rather than proactively.

Given their unwillingness to consider EC's members in aggregate rather than independently even at the present late stage, as was discussed above, this is hardly surprising. The reasons for this are difficult to establish, especially in the absence of recent empirical research on the subject. However, respondents in this study as well as the results of some earlier research point rather conclusively to a combination of two possible factors:

1.   The overall nature and relative lack of aggressiveness
      among Canadian managers and administrators, which was
      discussed in Chapter I; and
2.   The relatively low awareness about the EC among the
      Canadian public in general and among Canadian decision
      and policy makers in particular.
      An early study (Lasvergnas-Grémy et. al. 1976) showed
woefully low levels of awareness about either the EC itself or the
relative importance of Canada and the EC as trade partners,
among both the general public and among the "Professionals,
Managers, Administrators" occupational category. This was in
spite of the fact that the study was conducted fully 17 years after
the establishment of the EC and amid the broad media coverage
surrounding the signing of the Framework Agreement.

3.1.7. *The European View of Canada*
The interviews with European business and government
respondents do not bear out the prevailing Canadian view that,
at best, Canada's products have a neutral or non-existent image
in Europe. European attitudes about Canada are generally
positive. This partially stems from Canada's role in World War II
and from perceptions concerning its civility and neutrality,
domestically and internationally and both at the individual
citizen and at the government-political level. Respondents also
professed adequate knowledge about Canada's strengths in
engineering and technology along with surprise at the little
emphasis that Canadian manufacturers appear to place upon
European markets.

      A prime concern among those interviewed was, nonetheless,
the absence of Canadian-origin "flagship" industries which
might testify to Canadian technological competence and help to
spearhead export development in manufactures. This role is, for
instance, similar to the one played by German cars, Swiss
watches and American consumer products. These help to
promote, implicitly or explicitly, their respective countries'
strengths in engineering, precision instruments and marketing
technology. Although Canada does have several world-level
firms, most of them are not sufficiently visible or are frequently
thought of as American rather than Canadian. On the other
hand, those companies that represent exceptions to this rule (e.g.
Northern Telecom, Noranda, Molson and Labatt's, and some of
the major banks) are too few to generate the critical mass that the
term "flagship industry" implies.

3.2. Factors Affecting Canada's International Performance

Chapter I identified and discussed a number of factors that affect Canada's ability to compete in international markets. Although they are not unique to the Canadian-EC relationship, they are relevant to this study in the sense that they affect Canada's trade and FDI performance toward any developed market economy. The following points are discussed with reference to the corresponding topics in the first chapter (Section 3) of this essay.

The inconsistencies in Canadian policy are of special importance when they affect the interests of other, equally or more powerful, developed countries. This is especially significant in the case of Western Europe, where Canadian policies are often viewed on a comparative basis depending on their perceived impact upon European vs. U.S. interests. For example, FIRA was widely seen as particularly unfavourable to European investors while being more welcoming to U.S.-based corporations (interviews; also, see Twaalfhoven 1978). Regardless of whether this was true or not, the different perceptions of FIRA between European and U.S. investors were perhaps due to the larger distances involved (both geographically and culturally) in comparison with the U.S. and to the resulting difficulties in understanding and dealing with the agency. Needless to say, Canadian investors harbour similar complaints against various EC policies – often grounded on a similar lack of understanding because of distance and other factors.

Another general factor that has a specific effect on the Canada-EC relationship is the extent of foreign ownership in Canada. As mentioned, most Canadian plants of U.S. multinational firms are truncated subsidiaries. Their parent companies already have extensive operations in Western Europe. As a result, their interest in developing West European markets from their Canadian base is minimal at best.

This may explain why there is less interest today in the concept of "Global Product Mandating", which attracted a considerable amount of attention between 1979 and 1983 (e.g. see Rutenberg 1981; Rugman 1983). Some of the better known cases where world mandates were granted to Canadian subsidiaries by their multinational parents include Pratt and Whitney, Black and Decker, Westinghouse and General Electric. The optimism that followed these early cases became more cautious when it was realized that the number of firms planning to engage in this practice was very small, and that their overall impact on Canada would be equally small (Lilley 1983). U.S. respondents in this survey also pointed out that the significance of a world mandate to a subsidiary company is relatively small since the parent firm already has an international distribution network in place. This pre-existing network has two effects: it reduces the decision-making autonomy of the mandated branch, and it minimizes the experience that might otherwise be gained by having to engage in some typical international marketing activities (e.g. the search for foreign market opportunities, market selection, decisions on market entry methods, the development of strategies to penetrate foreign markets and the need to generate a foreign distribution network).

When coupled with the overall small size of Canadian industry, the concentration of foreign investment and trade in the hands of a small number of large firms, and the inward orientation of Canadian manufacturing due to its protected environment (see Chapter I), the level of foreign ownership in Canada therefore explains to a great extent the absence of a strong European orientation among Canadian-based enterprises.

Finally, the shortage of qualified managerial, engineering and research personnel is also a factor that acquires special significance when Canada's international competitiveness in developed markets is considered. The same is true in regards to the administrative orientation of many Canadian managers. The intense competition in markets such as those of the EC makes technological know-how and marketing skills more important than the country-specific comparative advantages that stem from resource ownership. The distinction that was made earlier (Chapter I) between "trade" and "marketing" is particularly relevant here.

Canadian corporations have been especially successful internationally in developing resource industries and markets, and in carrying out major turn-key contracts for large scale engineering projects (e.g. see Dagenais 1981 and Wright 1981). In both of these and in other similar cases, success often depends upon personal communication with high-ranking government or industry officials, frequently in Third World countries. This type of situation is vastly different, however, from attempts to penetrate highly competitive developed markets. The latter require specialized skills in areas such as international marketing and management, negotiations, finance, transnational production management, and others. Unfortunately, the educational and assistance infrastructure in Canada has not equipped Canadian corporations with these skills, which have helped their American, French, German, or Japanese counterparts to establish their competitive advantages in the international arena.

Notes

1. "End Products" are finished goods that fall mainly into five sub-categories: industrial machinery, agricultural machinery, transportation equipment (including passenger vehicles), other equipment and tools (e.g. for heating and refrigeration), and a variety of end-consumer products (e.g. footwear, toys). "Fabricated Materials" are processed goods that are used in the production of other goods and services; they also fall into five sub-categories: wood and paper, textiles, chemicals, iron and steel, and non-ferrous metals.

2. "Crude Materials" are essentially unprocessed goods; they range from raw or undressed hides and fur skins to metal ores and concentrates, precious metals, radioactive ores and petroleum.

3. The Airbus issue is largely "perceptual", in the sense that it stems from the different views held on each side of the Atlantic concerning the role of airlines. In Europe, most major airlines are state-owned and are seen as important elements in a country's sovereignty. Therefore, governments participate heavily in their airline companies' decisions as to which aircraft will be bought. Viewed from this perspective, it is not easy for the Europeans to understand the largely independent decision-making process of Canadian airlines. This is especially true in the case of Air Canada where, because it is a Crown corporation, government involvement in decision-making is expected to be heavier. The Canadian government's unwillingness to intervene is seen as reluctance to support a European product, rather than as a reflection of an altogether different type of relationship between the state and its enterprises (an interesting discussion of these issues can be found in Sampson 1984).

4. The term "Canadian-owned and controlled" is deliberately used here to exclude foreign- (mainly U.S.-) owned or controlled firms. Although some changes have since occurred (as a result, for example, of global product mandating), foreign firms were, and most still are, truncated subsidiaries (Barrows and Lyman 1975). Their operations are limited to supplying the domestic Canadian market or providing parts etc. to their foreign parents, and their interest (or capability) in exploring overseas markets is minimal or non-existent.

Chapter IV:

Canada and the European Community: Policy Issues for a More Comfortable Relationship

"The European Community is the largest unified market in the world, and we believe we can increase our business with it".

The Hon. James Kelleher
Minister for International Trade
London, U.K., February 1986

The three previous chapters reviewed the evolution and present status of the economic relationship between Canada and the European Community in terms of both trade and direct investment flows.

Chapter I discussed Canada's apparently thriving export trade but also highlighted some of the weaknesses that make it, along with the economy it supports, vulnerable in several ways. Special reference was made to those aspects that are particularly relevant to Canada's relationship with other developed market economies. Erratic government policies, shortcomings in the training of suitable personnel for today's business needs, the role of foreign-owned companies in external trade, and a protected business environment, were among the key factors that were identified as being instrumental in generating Canada's weaknesses in the international arena. The most important of these weaknesses are its minimal economic presence outside of North America and its heavy reliance on resources for a positive trade balance.

Chapter II reviewed the European Community. Three areas that are considered critical to the Canada-EC relationship were examined in some detail: the Community's strengths in trade and foreign direct investment, both internally and world-wide; the dangers arising for non-EC countries from the Community's efforts to conclude trade agreements with other countries or regions — most notably EFTA and the ACP countries; and the EC's prospects and future role in the world, both as a trading block and as an attempt at economic and political integration.

Chapter III drew from, and expanded upon, the discussion in Chapters I and II. It showed how a previously strong relationship declined almost continuously over the years and seems to be worsening today. This is despite the traditional friendship and good intentions that culminated in signing the Framework Agreement and that continue to exist. In attempting to identify the factors that caused these trends, it was suggested that the apparent shift in Canadian policy toward continentalism, the lack of political will on both sides, the slow growth of the European economy, the small size of the Canadian economy, wide-spread misunderstanding both in the EC and Canada about each other's needs, nature and role in the global environment, and some of the systemic weaknesses in Canada's external trade – all contributed to the present, mutually low levels of trade and investment.

The inescapable conclusion from the above discussion is that, at least at this point in time, the Canada-EC partnership is an uncomfortable one at best. In effect, the preceding chapters describe a paradox. This is the absence of a strong economic relationship despite the presence of a number of pre-conditions, ranging from geography and cultural affinity to a strong trade base in the early years, that would argue in the opposite direction.

What remains for this chapter is to attempt to identify the policy directions that seem to be worth exploring in order to achieve a reversal of the trend and a strengthening of the Canada-EC partnership – if any policies are deemed necessary at all.

This last qualifying phrase is important since policy-making and, especially, the implementation of policy are costly both in terms of commission (the cost of addressing a given issue) and in terms of omission (the opportunity cost from not addressing others because of resource limitations). To pursue policies that would strengthen Canada-EC trade would pre-suppose affirmative answers to two questions: Does Canada need to strengthen its external trade in general? If so, is the European Community an appropriate target for Canadian efforts in the trade and investment sphere?[1]

The answer to the first question appears almost redundant and is an unqualified yes. The early 1980s seem to have actually had a watershed effect on the attitudes of Canada's opinion leaders and policy-makers concerning the importance of external trade. As one expert on Canada-U.S. trade remarked to this researcher: "Until the late 1970s it was difficult to find a speaker who could address intelligently a conference on Canadian trade problems and so I was very much in demand; today there are hundreds of qualified experts – and I am still in demand because there are just as many conferences".

This may be an understatement. Indeed the number of special reports (many of which are included in the bibliography of this study) and public discussions or conferences, the amount of government attention and business involvement, and other indications of interest in trade, have all risen exponentially between 1980 and today. This interest may have its roots in the realization that Canada's share of world exports had been declining steadily or that exports appear to be a *sine qua non* in Canada's efforts to reduce its current account deficit:

> "The consensus among economic analysts is that Canada's current account deficit can only be corrected through a large and sustained increase in our merchandise trade surplus" (Voyer and Murphy 1984:27).

This realization may have been an important catalyst which led to the present widespread awareness on the importance of trade. Another possible catalyst, with the same effect, may have been Canada's drop from the sixth to eleventh position among 28 countries, between 1982 and 1983, in the European Management Forum's annual survey of industrial competitiveness[2]. This received widespread attention both in the mass media and in expert circles (e.g. see Science Council 1984:8 and The Canadian Economy 1983:24).

In view of the above, we can now turn to the second of the questions that were raised earlier. Is the European Community an appropriate target for Canadian trade and FDI development? If so, two relevant corollary questions are: What are the necessary considerations that must form the background of policy development toward this end, and what specific policy initiatives can be considered in this context?

1. Broadening Canadian Trade and FDI Destinations: The Case of the EC

Canada's largest trading partner is the United States. This will remain so and there is no foreseeable reason why it should not. One of the unfortunate elements in the "continentalism vs. diversification" debate over the years has been that the issue has often been perceived as a zero-sum game. As a result, when new trade areas have attracted policy attention, there has been a tendency in Canada to allow its interest in other destinations to wane. This should not be so. Notwithstanding an earlier comment about the cost involved in policy initiatives, it appears patently unreasonable to allow present relationships to wither in the pursuit of new ones.

It is in this light that the question of the EC as a possible policy target for Canada is viewed. The question can be seen from two opposite angles: Does the EC present sufficient export and investment *opportunities* to warrant policy attention on the part of Canada? Alternatively, can Canada *afford to neglect* its relationship with the EC in terms of policy emphasis?

1.1. The EC as an Opportunity

There are several factors that make the Community market an attractive one. These are often clouded under misunderstanding and lack of awareness about the key elements of both the Community as a whole and its individual members. Building on the data that were discussed in Chapters II and III, the following summary outlines some of these elements.

A recurring problem in assessments of the market potential of the EC has been the casual use of "market growth" and "market size" inter-changeably when discussing "market potential". "Market growth" arguments have been at the heart of the present emphasis on countries of the Pacific Rim. Such countries have an unquestionable growth potential, and Canada would be well advised to establish an early and strong presence in the region (unlike its failure to realize the internal growth potential of the EC in the 1950s, as was discussed earlier).

On the other hand, to downplay the significance of other large trading regions to the extent that Canada has with the EC carries the argument too far. Multinational firms, at least in the U.S., have for years been using both growth and size as indicators of market attractiveness, and a specific statistical technique (the "shift-share" method[3]) is available in the marketing literature for this purpose (Huff and Scherr 1967; Green and Allaway 1985). The comparative significance of growth and size can be seen in the following sample statistics:

a. Each share point of EC imports is worth approximately US$6 billion. Each share in Japan's imports is worth about US$1.3 billion. Canada's penetration of the Japanese market would therefore have to be five times as great as that of the EC market in order to generate the same net export effect for Canada.

b. Japan's GDP would have to grow two-and-a-half times as fast as that of the EC to generate the same net incremental growth in their respective economies.

c.   When all the less developed, non-CMEA (Council for Mutual Economic Assistance) countries of Asia are taken together, including the Pacific Rim, their present level of imports represents about one-third of total EC imports. Yet this group includes 32 countries, ranging from the People's Republic of China and India to Hong Kong, Singapore and 28 others.

d.   Finally, if Canada were to increase its share of EC imports from 1 per cent to 3 per cent, or to one-sixth of its level of penetration of the U.S. market, this would add US$12 billion to its current exports.

As can be seen from these examples, the import potential of the EC is substantial. Yet besides the confusion between growth rates and market size, three additional myths exist that tend to mask the Community's potential as an export destination. These have played an important role in shaping the present Canada-EC relationship and should be identified here.

First is the myth of market saturation. Based on the apparent abundance of goods and services in EC countries, many observers have failed to recognize the fact that, partly due to slow economic growth, most indicators (ranging from consumer ownership of durables to the degree of self-sufficiency in high-technology industrial products) stand at far lower levels than their Canadian equivalents (for some examples see European File 1980a and 1980b; Papadopoulos 1982c).

The second myth refers to the common misconception that external EC tariffs are too high; while this is true in comparison with the abolition of internal tariffs by the EC, it is not so in relation to most other industrialized countries – and certainly not in relation to Canada. The following figures show the average tariff schedules of selected countries for industrial imports (Economic Council 1983:98).

Country or Region	Tariff Average (after the Tokyo Round) %
EC	4.8
Canada	7.9
U.S.	4.4
Sweden	4.3
Norway	3.2
Switzerland	2.5
Austria	7.8
Finland	4.8
Japan	2.6
New Zealand	17.6

Naturally, the tariff average does not adequately reflect variations between sectors. These figures also do not account for the reality of non-tariff barriers which, in many cases, are significant (e.g. concerning automobile imports in Japan, textiles and clothing in Canada, agricultural products in the EC, and others). As was mentioned in Chapter II, however, the quotas, inter-market variations in standards and other technical requirements that are encountered within the EC are not much unlike those of Canada and its provinces or the U.S. and its states. More important, inter-country variations and non-tariff barriers among and in countries in the Pacific Rim, Latin America and other regions are significantly more pronounced than those within the EC (e.g. Salehizadeh 1983). In view of this, the second myth can be explained perhaps by the reality of exaggerated expectations against which European integration is being assessed, as noted earlier.

The third myth reflects the view that EC members are too different from one another to allow the realization of economies of scale through the development of common penetration strategies. This is true in many cases, including differing electrical equipment standards, differences in taste, culture and languages across Europe, etc. Yet the large number of standardized American, Japanese and other products that have been successfully marketed throughout the EC (indeed, the world) for several decades does not bear this argument out in the general case, when the exports of a given country — in this case Canada — are viewed on a sectoral or economy-wide basis (see also Papadopoulos 1982b).

In summary, although market rates in the EC are much slower than those in some other regions, the Community's internal markets are sufficiently large to warrant more attention on the part of Canada; if successful, increased efforts toward the EC could have a substantial positive impact upon the size of Canadian exports.

1.2. The EC as a Threat

The strong and growing presence of products, services and enterprises from the EC in world markets is a continuous threat to Canadian international firms. For example, in interviews with 28 executives from a large Canadian MNC in the field of telecommunications, it became apparent that its main threat in third markets (e.g. Middle East, Africa, Latin America) comes not so much from the U.S. and Japanese firms as from European ones such as Thomson, Ericsson, and Siemens. More generally, the fact that both partners perceive a strong need to enhance their presence in newer, higher technology areas poses a significant challenge for Canada, in view of the large size and competitive advantages of EC firms.

In addition to this challenge concerning new markets, the Community's agreements with third countries pose a growing threat against some of Canada's traditional export and FDI destinations. The decline of exports to the U.K., when it joined the EC, was already cited as a prime example of this threat. A more recent case is that of Canadian newsprint, where a problem arose because of the recent (1984) implementation of the final provisions of the EC's free trade agreements with the EFTA countries[4].

These agreements allow the importation of Scandinavian newsprint into the EC free of duty. As a result the Community imposed a quota on Canadian newsprint at 500,000 tons annually – down from the traditional level of approximately 700,000 tons (OECD 1984:44,38). Canada lodged a complaint and requested an investigation under the GATT, and the issue was resolved in December 1984 by settling the quota at 600,000 tons (*Globe and Mail* 27-05-1985:R1). This still represents a loss for Canada of seven share points from the EC's annual imports of newsprint.

This type of problem is likely to intensify as the EC expands its network of associations and agreements. Among the more recent ones, the EC-China agreement shows the potential conflict arising from both Canada's and EC's interests in the same new and growing markets. This agreement granted China special status under the Community's Generalized Preferences Scheme, liberalized 90 per cent of China's exports to the EC, and helped to quintuple EC exports to China between 1973 and 1983 (Leonard 1983).

This situation argues in favour of two types of pro-active, EC-focused policies. First are those that increase co-operation and reduce conflict in the general sense. The need for co-operation acquires special significance when Canada's position in the GATT is considered. For Canada, a principal function of the GATT has been ". . . to restrain and discipline the trade policies and practices . . . of larger countries . . ." (Stone 1984:209). However, as the author points out, the creation of the EC has resulted in ". . . a realignment of power relationships, which has diminished somewhat the role and influence of Canada within the [world] system" (p. 75). While a continuing commitment to multilateralism through the GATT is a must, therefore, the strengthening of Canada's bilateral relationship specifically with

major partners such as the U.S., the EC, and Japan also seems
necessary.

Second are policies which encourage foreign direct
investment in the EC. Outbound FDI is often opposed on the
grounds that "exports create jobs while [it] takes jobs away".
This argument, however, fails to recognize its important role in
spearheading exports from the investing company's home
country. The increasing importance of capital flows, in
comparison to traditional product flows, is one of the major post-
World War II international business phenomena. For example,
the Economic Council of Canada has stated that:

> "In this day and age both trade and foreign investment
> are but two sides of the same coin. The fact that over
> 50 per cent of Canada's trade in manufactured
> products with the United States is intra-firm furnishes
> ample evidence of the significance of this
> phenomenon." (1983:135).

Encouraging Canadian FDI in the EC could have many
beneficial effects for Canada. Most important, this would be an
effective means of maintaining access to, and reducing the risk of
losing, both EC markets as well as those with which the
Community has or may develop third-party agreements.

1.3. The EC as a Market for Canada: Conclusion

The recent federal government paper on "Competitiveness and
Security" for Canada (The Right Hon. Joe Clark 1985:15) states
that "it remains a priority objective to enlarge our market share
[in Europe], particularly for manufactured goods". The priority
appears to be well-placed and it will hopefully be put into
operation. The preceding discussion suggests that it should[5]. As
Hudson, Rhind and Mounsey (1984:139) have pointed out, in
attempting to answer the question of whether the EC is an
"emerging superpower",

> "from the evidence presented in the preceding
> chapters, there are reasonable grounds for arguing
> that it has indeed attained such a status, particularly
> as regards the size and sophistication of its economy".

Although the precise strength of the EC in the future is open
to argument, and some would find the above statement an
exaggeration, it does point to a reality that seems to be almost
universally recognized: that the EC *is* indeed a force in the

international economic sphere. To suggest that its slow economic growth in the recent past makes it undeserving of policy attention would be as myopic as to suggest less emphasis on the Pacific Rim because of small market sizes, or to pursue policies aimed exclusively at diversification, which would be at the expense of Canada's strong trade relationship with the United States.

2. Background Factors in Canadian Policy Development

Recognizing that a problem exists and defining its nature are the most important steps toward its solution. As a first step in developing and discussing policy alternatives, therefore, it is necessary to define the dimensions of the present and future challenges to Canada's international competitive position. Many of these have already come to the forefront in the intense trade-related activity and thinking of the early 1980s.   Others, unfortunately, have not. Both types must be summarized here, so that they can serve as a background to the next and final section in this essay.

2.1. Increasing Competition in Resources

The significant challenge arising from the increase in the amount and intensity of global competition in natural resources, ranging from agriculture and fisheries to ores and minerals, seems to be recognized by all concerned.   This challenge is especially important to Canada, since it concerns its area of traditional comparative advantage.

Increasing competition in this area is largely a result of the rising foreign debt of many countries in the Third World, and of their need to industrialize through export development. Given their weakness in manufacturing, the attention of these countries focuses by necessity on resource exports[6]. The measures undertaken to encourage such exports are many and varied but, in the absence of indigenous expertise, they often focus on attracting foreign investors who can develop the resources for export. Such measures range from the granting of tax holidays and the establishment of export processing zones, to special incentive programs and, occasionally, dumping.

This poses a substantial two-fold challenge to Canada's traditional comparative advantage in world markets (OECD 1984:38). First, when the efforts of less developed nations to attract investment in resources are successful, this investment is lost to other potential hosts – including Canada. Second, the undifferentiated nature of most basic commodities, along with increases in supply, result in suppressing their prices in world markets. In turn, this often generates an immediate negative effect on some of Canada's mainstay exports. Examples of these effects over the recent past include the price fluctuations in commodities ranging from nickel and oil to gold and uranium.

2.2. Increasing Competition in Advanced Technology

Turning to another, also widely-recognized, challenge it can be said that Canada's drive toward strengthening its advanced technology exports is also at risk. The danger here arises from the fact that advanced technology is precisely the locus of emphasis of practically all other industrialized countries. The U.S., Japan and most of the major EC states are fiercely competing to establish their future strengths in order to fuel growth and prevent the stagnation of their economies. Some of the sectors where Canada is likely to face major competitive challenges are aerospace, telecommunications and urban transit systems.

2.3. New Elements in International Trade and Investment

The need to develop contemporary means of handling foreign trade and investment seems to be receiving some belated but well-deserved attention. These range from world product mandating (notwithstanding the fact that it holds less promise than originally thought; see above) to counter-trade (Science Council 1984:43), trading houses (Canada's Trade Challenge 1982) and free trade zones (Grubel 1983).

Regardless of the final direction that such initiatives may take, and of the arguments surrounding the various possible directions, the fact that they are being discussed is a hopeful sign. This is so because Canada's delay in adopting these new approaches to foreign trade and investment may have already placed it at a competitive disadvantage, both generally and specifically in relation to the EC.

For example, there are more than 100 free trade zones in each of Western Europe, the U.S., and the Newly Industrialized Countries today. These have attracted investors who might otherwise have chosen Canada as a host country. Specific cases that demonstrate this possibility include Germany's BMW and Volkswagen, and Italy's Olivetti, all of which established major manufacturing and/or distribution plants in U.S. free trade zones. As of this writing, Canada has established two such zones (in Stephenville and Sydney, in 1984), but neither has yet attracted significant numbers of tenants (Papadopoulos 1985).

2.4. Weakness in Manufacturing

With few exceptions, trade and investment experts agree that there is a need to strengthen the performance of the manufacturing sectors of the Canadian economy, both domestically and in international markets. Currently, the trade balance is positive mostly in sectors where the research and development input is low, and negative in most sectors that have a high research component (Voyer and Murphy 1984:31, 152). In addition to the low growth rates and intense competition that will characterize the international resource markets in the future, Voyer and Murphy have also shown (p. 35) that additional emphasis on resources can have serious detrimental effects on Canada's physical environment. Therefore, the present emphasis on encouraging exports of manufactured goods can have a significant and beneficial impact on future export development and on the Canadian economy overall.

While the importance of the above four dimensions seems to be widely recognized in Canada today, that of others is not. This does not mean that they are totally absent from the vocabulary of those interviewed or from the literature and public policy reports. Rather, these factors have either been paid only lip-service, or they have remained at the public rhetoric level, or they are being recognized by only a small (though often vocal) minority. These are discussed below.

2.5. Need for a Geopolitical Perspective

A most important consideration is the need to adopt a geopolitical perspective on world trade. The problem has been put in rather strong terms: "Academic economists and businessmen here have a parish mentality. They have no understanding of what's going on in the world" (see Davies 1983:48). The uniqueness of such a perspective is that it considers the global environment from a multiplicity of dimensions. These include the incorporation of both economic and political determinants, and of both size and growth rate factors, in attempting to identify the present status and future potential of important actors in the international scene.

A geopolitical perspective would place primary emphasis on the U.S., the EC, the Pacific Rim and Eastern Socialist countries. The order of these regions in terms of importance would of course vary depending on which country's perspective is being discussed. In Canada, the importance of some of these regions (e.g. the U.S. and the Pacific Rim) is being acknowledged but that of others receives significantly less attention. The significance of the EC was noted above, and so was its potential function as a bridge to Eastern Europe (which is likely to play a much more active role in foreign trade and investment in the years to come).

Further, the present emphasis in Canadian policy and business decision making on the Pacific Rim fails to recognize the challenge posed by the strong presence of Japanese, Taiwanese, Korean and U.S. interests in that region. The first three of these nations dominate trade and investments in countries like Singapore and China, while the U.S. is particularly strong in Japan itself, the Philippines and some other countries. These countries, and the companies that represent them, are unlikely to relinquish their competitive advantages in the region. Thus, while Canadian emphasis on the Pacific Rim is well-warranted and should continue, the expectation that it will emerge into a dominant market may be exaggerated. In turn, this would argue for sustaining, if not enhancing, what little strength Canada now has in Europe — both West and East.

2.6. Penetrating DME vs. LDC Markets

Trade and investment are vastly different propositions where DME versus LDC destinations are concerned. The comparative ease of penetrating the U.S. market, because of its similarities with Canada, and of trading with LDCs and Eastern Europe in resources and agriculture, have not prepared Canadian corporations to conduct business competitively with, or in, the major developed markets of Europe or the Pacific Rim.

As noted earlier, success in such markets (and especially in the EC) requires strong managerial and technical skills and would suggest a more aggressive and competitive orientation toward external trade and investment. Yet as pointed out repeatedly both in the interviews and in the literature, with few exceptions (e.g. the major banks and some firms in the high technology and beverage sectors), Canadian companies have not been eager or able to develop the requisite skills and the overall market orientation that have been the cornerstones of success for Japanese and American companies in Western Europe and in other DME markets. It is interesting to note that Canadian business people themselves appear to agree on this point. In a variety of studies, exporters have listed "product quality" and "performance" among their key strengths, and "marketing" or "finance" among their main weaknesses (e.g. Beamish, Goerzen and Munro 1984; Kaynak 1981).

2.7. Support for Increased Policy Emphasis on the EC

An essential ingredient in developing effective public policies is the presence of support by both public opinion and, of course, the constituency at which it is aimed. Only circumstantial evidence is available in this respect. Nonetheless, in the absence of research directly related to this subject, it may be useful to cite here some data which suggest, at least, the absence of any substantial opposition to developing closer economic links with the EC.

For example, even amid the generally "pro-continentalist" mood of the mid-1980s, support for closer ties with Europe is not insignificant. Based on a national sample of 3,069 respondents, LeDuc and Murray (1984:137) found a 37-34-20 split between preferences for moving "closer to the U.S.", "staying as we are", and moving "closer to Europe", respectively, in 1983. Although the "pro-European" proportion is sufficiently high, it could be hypothesized that it might rise even higher if the common misunderstanding about the mutually exclusive nature of the various options did not exist (as discussed above).

Further, business interest in Community markets has remained relatively strong, in spite of the overall deterioration in Canada-EC trade and investment. On a country basis, Japan continues to attract more attention in Canada than individual members of the EC. However, research shows that "Western Europe" and/or the EC are the preferred destination regions by Canadian exporters following the U.S. In fact, Beamish, Goerzen and Munro (1984) show that 89 per cent, 26 per cent, and 20 per cent of the *firms* in their sample serve, respectively, the U.S., British and West European markets (multiple responses). Japan was reported as an export destination by only 9 per cent of the sample, and this was lower than the proportions mentioned for Central America, the Middle East and several other regions. Similar findings have been reported by several other Canadian researchers (e.g. Crookell and Caliendo 1979; Kaynak 1981).

It should be noted that the above figures represent *numbers of firms* rather than volume of trade. This can help explain the apparent discrepancy between these findings and the statistical evidence with shows ever-increasing trade *volumes* with Japan, along with a proportionate decline of the importance of the EC in Canadian exports. In attempting to understand this discrepancy, it is necessary to recall three points made earlier in this essay: first, that Canada is one of the few countries whose exports have increased steadily over the recent past; second, that the average size of Canadian exporting firms is small; and third, that a large proportion of Canadian exports to Japan (71 per cent) is

accounted for by only nine Japanese trading companies in
Canada (Ch. I, Section 3.2.1). Coupled with the above findings,
these three points suggest the following:

a.   The growth in exports to Japan largely reflects that
     country's need for resources (which it imports through the
     Canadian subsidiaries of some of its major trading
     companies) rather than a commensurate amount of interest
     on the part of indigenous Canadian firms. As a result, these
     exports over-represent the apparent preference of Canadian
     companies for the Japanese market and are subject to the
     continuing commitment of Japanese firms to source these
     commodities in Canada. As noted in section (2.1) above,
     though, this commitment may well be contingent upon the
     availability of comparable but less expensive commodities
     from other suppliers in LDCs.

b.   The deterioration of the EC's relative importance in
     Canadian exports may greatly under-represent the amount
     of interest in that market on the part of Canadian firms.
     The present low proportion of exports to the EC can be
     partially attributed to the overall growth in total Canadian
     exports, and to the fact that the majority of exports to the
     EC seem to be made by smaller firms and are thus lower in
     volume on an individual basis. Stated differently: although
     exports to the EC have been declining on a percentage basis,
     they still represent a large volume ($7 billion; see Table
     XVI) and they are of paramount importance to many
     Canadian exporters.

2.8. Directions in Public Policy

Another important prerequisite in improving Canada's economic
links with the EC is the recognition of the nature of the
limitations of earlier public policies. A few examples, building
upon those that were discussed in Chapter I, can help make this
point.

a   Government programs developed to encourage and support
     external trade have tended to substitute for, rather than
     assist, entrepreneurial drive and innovativeness, thus
     creating a dependency of the private sector on government
     for functions that clearly fall within the domain of the
     former (The Canadian Economy 1983:27; also Papadopoulos
     1982a).

b.   Policies have often been prescribed without concern for the
     systemic limitations that would hamper their
     implementation. For example, non-U.S. foreign investors
     have been encouraged to invest in Canada – and then left to

fend for themselves amid a tangle of federal and provincial jurisdictional problems ranging from business issues (e.g. incentives programs) to problems concerning the investing companies' expatriate personnel (e.g. regarding immigration and schooling of foreign executives' family members; see Wright 1984:81; also von Franque 1986).

c. Industrial assistance programs (such as the variety of research and innovation centres established to support the high technology industry) have addressed entire sectors at the general level, with little regard to the particular needs of sub-sectors within them. The high technology sector is a very relevant example here. It includes a wide variety of industries ranging from computers and electronics to telecommunications, aerospace, biotechnology and others. All of these fall under the "high technology" umbrella, yet each has highly unique needs (see, for instance, Hay 1984; and the Hon. Frank Oberle 1986).

d. In pursuing closer relations with the U.S., the EC or the Pacific Rim at different times, Canada has often created friction in its relationships with its "left-out" partners (Daly 1981b).

e. Finally, public policy has failed to recognize the importance of outward direct investment as a forerunner in export development; trade and inward investment have virtually monopolized attention, and many Canadian multinational firms have been quietly ceded, *de facto* if not *de jure,* to other countries.

2.9. *Limitations of Canadian Management*

The unique characteristics of the Canadian psyche, as they affect the behaviour of private sector executives and the corporations they manage, do not seem to have been taken into account in policy development. The basic deficiencies in qualified and outward-oriented personnel have been masked behind the comfortable oasis of the resource trade surplus and behind unfavourable exchange rates as excuses for the inability or the lack of need to perform better in manufacturing.

Yet, as was indicated above, the impact of unfavourable exchange rates becomes severe especially when the very foundations of trade are not solid enough. Further, Canada's strength in resources cannot last forever — whether for competitive or physical and environmental reasons (see, for example, Macdonald Royal Commission 1985:Ch. 13). The need to emphasize "competence in doing" rather than "competence from owning" was already stressed above. Can Canadian industry make the shift? Voyer and Murphy have pointed out that "... as the Japanese have shown the world, comparative advantage can be engineered!" (1984:137). Some recent successes in the telecommunications, data processing, defence and other sectors, along with the basic fact that Canada is, after all, the seventh largest industrialized nation in the world, suggest that it can certainly succeed in enhancing its domestic and international competitiveness in manufacturing.

2.10. Summary

The above paragraphs outline the basic dimensions that help determine the nature of the challenge facing Canada in terms of maintaining and improving its international competitive strength. Along with the previous sections of this essay, these paragraphs suggest that the potential of the European Community as a trade and investment partner for Canada may warrant more attention than it now receives. Against this background, the next section examines possible policy directions that may contribute to the overall international competitiveness objective, through the development of closer economic links with the European Community.

3.   Some Policy Directions for a Stronger Canada-EC Partnership

Many of the policy initiatives that may be appropriate in developing closer economic ties with the European Community are common to Canada's need to compete more effectively in and against all developed market economies. Stated differently, some of the measures that appear necessary to improve the Canada-EC trade and investment relationship are also likely to have, as a by-product, a beneficial effect on Canada's relationship with other developed countries (e.g. U.S., Japan) as well. On the other hand, some policy alternatives are unique to the Canada-EC relationship. Each is discussed in a separate section below.

3.1. General Policies

Assuming that the considerations mentioned earlier have been or will be internalized, a number of policies can help achieve Canada's international competitiveness goal. Competition can be seen in two ways: trade and investment *toward or from DMEs,* and trade and investment toward third countries *in competition with* other DMEs.

3.1.1.   *Understanding Competitive Forces*

A first task in understanding competition would be to attempt to ascertain the relative positions of major regions and countries of the world and, perhaps more important, to determine the role of Canada in this context. This would be in line with the geopolitical perspective that was discussed above, as well as with the concept of competitive positioning, which is of paramount importance in international marketing.

The concept of competitive positioning, aiming at an assessment of other competitors' strength, has been at the forefront of private sector thinking for over 15 years. Positioning is based on "perceptual mapping". This attempts to determine the way buyers perceive the comparative strengths and weaknesses of alternative sellers. In commercial marketing, this concept is an integral part in the development of competitive strategies and often requires substantial expenditures on buyer research. Yet, this concept is almost totally foreign to policy making.

The literature in Canada is replete with references to the way *Canadians* think about how foreign buyers and investors perceive the country, its people and its industrial strengths and weaknesses. References to Canada's image as a "resource hinterland" (Voyer and Murphy 1984:37) or to Canadian executives' image as hard to negotiate with (interviews with Canadian officials in Europe) are typical examples in this case. Yet this country has never attempted to undertake a systematic assessment of its image among *foreign buyers*[7]. Interviews in this study point to the distinct possibility of a wide divergence between Canada's perception of itself and other peoples' perceptions of Canada. What is needed, then, is the undertaking of formal marketing research in a variety of countries representing Canada's key trade interests, with the objective of assessing the country's image among its target buyers.

Further, what is not known is the nature of Canada's image abroad in terms of its relationship to the U.S. Hypotheses (by Canadians) range from Canada being seen as a strongly independent country with clearly different policy goals and behavior than those of the U.S., all the way to a Canadian image as totally indistinct and indistinguishable from that of the U.S.

A systematic assessment in this area could become an important policy task that would enable Canada to position itself internationally in relation to its strengths. Such an assessment would involve three broad steps: first , the operationalization of the above-mentioned geopolitical perspective, aimed at determining the present and future strengths of various regions and DMEs; second, an investigation of Canada's perceived image in high-potential regions (those identified in the preceding step). This would be based upon perceptual mapping, with special emphasis on perceptions about Canada's areas of competence and about its relationship with the United States. Finally, the third step would involve a policy decision as to the desired positioning of Canadian products in foreign markets, based on the two previous steps.

3.1.2. Trade Development Model

A second major decision would refer to the export development model upon which Canada would base the development of policy. At least four models can be considered here. The first is that of the U.S., which is primarily based on the concept of minimal government involvement and maximal reliance on aggressive marketing by the private sector. Second is the Japanese model, which is based on heavy government involvement along with the fostering of aggressive international marketing through large industrial and trading complexes. Third is the European Community model, which is based on a combination of a strong relationship between the government and industrial establishments, the encouragement of international marketing and the development of an ever-larger "internal" trade area through associations with other countries or regions. Finally, a fourth alternative would be a uniquely Canadian model, which, however, would probably reflect elements from all of the preceding three.

Canadian policy has vacillated in this regard between the "free enterprise" and "public program" extremes. On the one hand, programs and organizations such as the NEP, FIRA, the agricultural marketing boards, Petro-Can and the Export Development Corporation (EDC) show a preference for the second of these extremes. On the other hand, Canada's support for export development is lower than that of most other countries. For example, the proportion of exports receiving government support is less than 1 per cent in Canada but stands at about 4 per cent for the U.S., 8 per cent for Japan and West Germany, 12 per cent for the U.K., and 13 per cent for France (Economic Council data quoted in Voyer and Murphy 1984:16)[8,9].

Having decided upon an appropriate model for Canada, steps could be taken to operationalize it. The specific steps lie beyond the scope of this discussion but would range from encouraging the development of large industries through incentives for mergers among domestic or between domestic and foreign enterprises (along the EC model, as exemplified by

Airbus) all the way to a withdrawal of government support in most areas except, perhaps, financing and risk insurance for major international undertakings.

3.1.3. Other Issues

The third general policy area covers a broad range of issues that were addressed at various points in this essay but are too numerous to treat individually here. These include the need to enlarge the qualified personnel pool in certain disciplines for Canadian industry, to encourage a stronger outward orientation on the part of private sector leaders, to address those irritants (e.g. immigration, education, regional incentives, regional differences) that negatively affect foreign investors' perceptions about Canada, to strengthen the country's manufacturing sector, and many others. There are two common elements among the policies that fall in this category.

First, all are necessary prerequisites if Canada is to succeed in its drive to enhance its international competitiveness in and against DMEs. To capture a larger share of the EC market, or to compete effectively for telecommunications projects against Sweden's Ericsson in, say, Senegal, what Canadian corporations need is capital, personnel, know-how, and an appropriate image, more so than a comparative advantage in resources at home (see also Macdonald Royal Commission 1985:239). Without these, Canada's prospects for maintaining or strengthening its position in world markets are doubtful at best.

Second, they all reflect the need for co-ordination and consistency in public policy development. The vacillations and temporal inconsistencies of Canadian policy that were identified at various points in this essay do nothing but waste resources, create opportunity costs, reduce the country's international effectiveness and damage its international reputation.

3.2. EC-Specific Policies
3.2.1. Need for Community-wide Strategies

The first and most important policy consideration is the need to acknowledge the importance, not to mention the very existence, of the EC as *one entity*. This, as already noted, has been a major ingredient in the success of U.S. companies, which view their exact location within the EC as secondary to their ability to access the entire market from any location inside it (see also Haex et al. in Pelkmans 1983).

This must not be taken to imply that bilateral relations with individual EC members are not important. Rather, it emphasizes the fact that for many trade and investment matters, and from the general policy perspective, the EC plays a different role than that of its members. As a Community official responding to this study put it during an interview at the Commission's headquarters in Brussels, "the EC is *not equal to* or *larger than* the sum of its parts; the EC *is different than* the sum of its parts".

Areas where the EC's influence is strongest include its jurisdiction on quotas and some non-tariff barriers, the establishment of general health and safety standards that apply across the Community, sectoral matters and negotiations (such as countervail measures in cases where EC interests are, or are perceived to be, threatened), certain issues in international policy (and politics), and the administration and enforcement of the common policies concerning agriculture, competition, and consumer protection.

An example at this point can help clarify the role of the EC as a separate entity. Let us assume a Canadian firm exports to or invests in France and Germany. The company naturally operates under the impression that it is dealing solely with French and German government or industry officials, respectively. In operating in these two countries it will probably never encounter an EC official or become involved in Community law *per se*.

This, however, creates what is to some extent an illusion. Chances are that many (though certainly not all) of the French and German policies or limitations that the company encounters have been decided upon at the Community level. They are thus likely to be encountered, with small variations, in all EC members. The operative distinction here is that on many trade and investment matters it is common EC policies, rather than country-specific ones, that are administered through the national governments (which have, of course, participated in developing the former).

Alternately, in those areas (and several do exist) where French or German policies deviate substantially from one another and from those of the EC, the Canadian exporter or investor is faced with the same conditions as those that would have existed in the absence of the Community. In this latter case, the Community's influence is manifested in a different way: once it has incorporated in one EC country, the Canadian firm can conduct business anywhere else in the EC while under the protection of the intra-Community provisions for the liberalization of trade.

An interesting example of a successful EC-wide strategy has been provided by Lumonics, a Canadian laser manufacturer. The company made substantial inroads into the Community with its laser-marking equipment by capitalizing on a consumer protection policy (requiring "best before" dates on dairy products) which was adopted and implemented across the EC starting in 1981[10].

At the policy level, closer ties with the Community would imply the need for EC-wide analysis and decision making. This would involve, but would not be limited to, first, the development of appropriate organizational structures with strong EC bureaus (rather than present "Western Europe" emphasis) both at the federal and provincial levels; second, the encouragement of EC-level consultations (e.g. compared to Canada's lukewarm activities at this level, the Chinese sent no less than 100 top decision-makers, led by China's Vice-Premier, to a meeting in Brussels with more than 400 leading EC firms and banks); third, the re-consideration of Canada's decision to withdraw from the Business Co-operation Centre in Brussels; fourth, the generation of EC-wide statistical data and analysis in Canada, for the benefit of both public policy and business decision makers[11]; and finally, the development of expertise on the EC by federal and provincial policy makers.

3.2.2. Market Access

Another important policy area is that of securing market access for Canadian firms and products in Europe. Traditionally this has been a thorny area in Canada-EC relations, in spite of the Framework Agreement. To a large extent, the lack of co-operation in this area is the result of the suspicions of each partner about the other on the question of protectionism, to mutual misunderstandings about the real nature of each other's policies, to the EC's mistrust of Canada because of its close ties with the U.S., and to Canada's mistrust of the EC because of both the internal protection it affords its own industries and the preferential access it allows to its associates (e.g. EFTA).

There are, however, enough case histories which suggest that co-operation can be both possible and very fruitful for both partners when the appropriate guidance and willingness to take action is present. Some recent examples include joint ventures in aerospace and other high technology sectors, such as the LLAD System which includes companies from Canada, the U.S., Switzerland, and Italy (*MacLean's* 1986:SR-1f); the arrangements made for the airing of French Canadian television programming in France (*Globe and Mail* 1986); and the Canada-France-West Germany agreement, with Canadair as the principal contractor, to develop certain types of military surveillance equipment (*Citizen* 1986).

Therefore, improvements in market access could be the result of negotiations that would draw strength from the potential benefits to both partners, arising from stronger trade and investment ties (such as, for example, the fisheries agreement). For Canada, the EC represents a potentially lucrative market which can also enhance its access to several third countries. At the same time, the Community represents a large complementary market that would help reduce (rather than substitute for) Canada's interdependence with the U.S. For the EC, Canada can provide a technologically advanced and resource-rich environment which also allows easy access to the U.S. market at little political risk. Further, and in addition to the non-negligible size of its own market, Canada can provide the Community with an access bridge to many countries in the Pacific Rim.

3.2.3. Specific Benefits
These last points can be especially significant in view of the apparently prevailing perception in Canada that its market is too small to be of interest to European firms. In turn, this has occasionally been used to explain the deteriorating Canada-EC relationship, on the grounds that the former has little to offer in return for better access to the market of the latter. This reasoning, however, tends to place too much emphasis on market size and pays too little attention to other benefits that may be of interest to foreign business. These other benefits can be both tangible and intangible, and capitalizing upon them can become an important target in policy making.

For example, a series of tangible benefits arising from Canada's geographic location may be of importance to European businesses wishing to trade with countries in the Pacific Rim. These include the fact that Canada has immediate access to both the Atlantic and Pacific oceans, an excellent overland transportation system and, as a Pacific Basin nation, considerable experience with and ties in Far Eastern countries. As a matter of policy, and in order to promote these benefits to potential European investors, Canada could establish a free trade zone on the west coast.

With the zones that already exist in Newfoundland and Nova Scotia, this would allow European firms to import raw or semi-finished materials into Canada free of duty, and to process them here for eventual re-export to the Pacific Rim. To the foreign investor, the benefits from such an arrangement would range from the ability to operate in the technologically advanced environment of Canada to obtaining easy access to important target markets. To Canada, the benefits would include increased foreign investment inflows, employment, technology transfer and the projection of a pro-trade attitude.

3.2.4. Infrastructure

Another relevant aspect of policy is the need for a special commercial infrastructure in Canada that would be capable of arming its industry for the effective penetration of EC markets. These markets are among the most advanced DMEs. The successful development of a presence in the Community, therefore, presupposes strong marketing skills and a strong manufacturing orientation. Canada lacks the first and, though well developed domestically, has international weaknesses in terms of the second. This calls for policies aimed at improving these conditions.

The nature of such policies is as far-reaching as it is self-evident. These could include support for educational programs both at the university level and through executive re-training seminars; the encouragement of research to foster a better understanding of the nature, limitations and strengths of managerial talent in Canada; and technical support for new product development in high-potential industries. Action has already been taken in some of these areas in recent years; this includes the establishment of five centres for international business at Canadian universities, the establishment of the Ontario Centre for Microelectronics, and seminars offered by various trade associations (e.g. the Canadian Manufacturers' Association).

However, these programs are relatively few and, all too often, tactics- rather than strategy-oriented. Tactical issues (e.g. export documentation or financing sources) certainly warrant the attention they receive. On the other hand, the discussion in this essay has, it is hoped, demonstrated the need for increased emphasis on questions of strategy. Thus, two types of programs seem to be necessary: those that will assist Canadian businesses in overcoming technical barriers to international activity; and those that will help them generate a strategic perspective on the need to internationalize, to understand the nature of foreign competition and to develop effective approaches for the penetration of foreign markets in terms of marketing, production, finance and human resource management considerations.

3.2.5. Encouraging Foreign Direct Investment

The nature of the EC market suggests that an important component of Canadian policy toward it should emphasize direct

investment significantly more than is now the case. The
Community's external tariff and non-tariff barriers, coupled with
the reality of its free trade agreements with EFTA, the ACP
countries, and other regions, point to the need for substantial
direct investment in Europe. Exactly how such investment can
materialize is beyond the limits of this discussion; this could take
the form of bilateral negotiation at the EC-Canada level or, at
least on the part of Canada, the granting of tax incentives, risk
insurance, capital financing and other kinds of support to firms
that wish to expand into the EC.

While the exact method is not important in this discussion,
the realization that direct investment in (and from) the EC must
become the subject of policy development, is not. In addition to
the above-mentioned advantages of such an orientation, it is
useful to recall here the point made earlier about the relative
strength of EC-based multinationals. In view of their dominant
role in many high-technology sectors (e.g. telecommunications,
aerospace), it is likely that their presence in Canada or the
presence of Canadian investment in the EC can benefit both
Canadian and European companies in at least three ways:
technology and knowledge transfer, the development of new
research opportunities, and the possibility of co-operation efforts
toward third markets[12].

3.2.6. "Flagship Industries" in Trade Development

The discussion throughout the preceding pages points to the need
for increased trade development activity by Canada in the EC. It
is not necessary to elaborate on the form that such activities
might take; from trade missions to trade fair support, and from
financing to sectoral promotions, these are well known and many
are already in place (although most often emphasizing other
destinations) or were examined above. Before concluding this
essay, however, it seems worthwhile to return to a point that was
discussed briefly in order to stress the major role it can play in
export development. This is the issue of the potentially adverse
effects arising from the absence of Canadian "flagship"
industries.

This issue is examined last although it is not perceived to be
least in importance. The experience of countries like Japan, the
U.S. and Switzerland has amply demonstrated how a handful of
successful sectors can spearhead export development in a number
of others. More recently, there has been considerable discussion
in North America about how one product, Hyundai's "Pony"
automobile, helped "catapult" an entire country onto international markets. Unlike any of its previous exports, the Pony

appears to have given South Korea the credibility and reputation it needs as a capable producer of branded, relatively advanced products, to further promote the entire range of its manufactured exports.

If the generally held assumption that Canada is mainly viewed as a resource-oriented country is correct (and there is no data to suggest otherwise), this can be a severe handicap to the successful development of any of the above policies. Generally, buyers around the world grow up with a variety of consumer products of foreign origin and form a preference for them. These preferences may later translate into perceptions about, or be reinforced through experiences with, industrial products. Compared with the strong loyalty that the products of many other countries enjoy, there are precious few branded, differentiable goods that a Canadian manufacturing reputation can be built upon at the present time.

A phrase that is frequently heard in exporters' circles in recent years is "Give us more Canadarms!" It is perhaps ironic that in the one market where Canada is exceptionally strong, the U.S., many of its products are indistinguishable from American ones and often go unnoticed, because of the cultural and language similarity. Concerning the European Community, it would seem necessary that a small number of sectors, products, or firms, capable of acting as Canadian "flagships", be encouraged to do so. This would involve identifying foreign product-market combinations where a substantial impact can be made, and then assisting (e.g. through tax or research grants) the appropriate Canadian sectors which could deliver it.

It would be a mistake to believe that such sectors can only be found where Canada's traditional comparative advantage lies – i.e. in resources. Canada has strong but little understood advantages that stem from the nature of the country itself. These include expertise in transportation and communications systems; in urban transit systems; in environmental protection; in water treatment systems; in aerospace; or in handling problems under extreme weather conditions. Having selected appropriate industries, it would then become a matter of policy implementation to encourage them to develop a strong presence in the EC through various forms of direct (e.g. trade promotions) or indirect (e.g. financing) means.

This is obviously a long-term undertaking, not unlike that which brought Japanese industry from its unknown status of four decades ago to its present strong position around the world. Nonetheless, the need to engage in it and the benefits that can accrue to Canada if it is successful are too important to go unmentioned.

Conclusion

The above analysis suggests that, while not de-emphasizing its U.S. relationship or decelerating its thrust toward the Pacific Rim, Canada must not allow its trade and investment ties with the EC to deteriorate any further. It has been argued that a geopolitical perspective would suggest that strong efforts must be undertaken to reverse the deterioration and to strengthen Canada's presence in the EC and the Community's presence in Canada. It is only through strong political will, and by the application of policies such as those outlined above, that the "uncomfortable partnership" between Canada and the European Community can become a more satisfying and better developed relationship for the benefit of both.

Notes

1. At the official level, the Community remains a "priority market" for Canada (see above). Nonetheless, the discussion that follows is deemed necessary because there are few, if any, manifestations of operationalization of this official view.

2. By 1984, Canada was back to seventh position (*Citizen* 15-01-85). However, this was due more to changes in the method of computing country standings than to real changes in Canada's competitive position. What is important is that Canada's position reflects its strengths in resources and finance, where it ranks among the top three nations. Instead, the country ranks lower on criteria such as "industrial unrest", and among the lowest-ranked countries (total in the survey: 28) on indicators such as productivity growth, size of government, and the tax burden.

3. The shift-share approach calculates a country's potential based on a comparison between (a) its absolute growth over a given period and (b) its expected growth, as reflected by the average growth rate of a "basket" of similar countries. The aim of the method is to calculate "net" and "per cent" shift, which would show the country's share, in absolute and

proportionate terms, in the total growth of the basket countries.

4. As noted elsewhere in the essay, this agreement liberalizes trade between the EC and EFTA countries. It is interesting to point out here that, in many quarters, this agreement is seen as a preamble for the *de facto* complete association between the two entities. In view of present levels of co-operation, and of the degree of integration among the economies involved, both sides are already being forced to consult on many issues that are not part of the formal agreement (see, for example, Lugon 1985). Should a complete association occur, the EC-EFTA combination would represent 18 nations comprising the vast majority of Western Europe.

5. The reader may note that in this statement, as well as in many other formal government statements, reference is made to "Europe" rather than to the EC.

6. This paragraph does not refer, of course, to those newly industrialized countries (e.g. South Korea, Brazil) which have developed noticeable manufacturing strengths in sectors such as automobiles, shipbuilding, or electronic products.

7. The terms most often used in relation to this type of research are "the country-of-origin effect" and "the made-in image". About 40 such studies have been published to date, but none has tested for Canada as an origin among foreign buyers. Nonetheless, interest in country-of-origin research has begun to emerge in Canada as well. Heslop and Wall (1985) have studied the "made-in" images of foreign products among Canadian consumers; further, results of a large-scale cross-national study about Canadian goods among consumers in eight countries, completed in 1986, have started to be published (see Papadopoulos and Heslop 1986; Papadopoulos, Heslop, Graby, and Avlonitis 1986).

8. The percentages represent "direct credits disbursed and guaranteed credits approved".

9. The present government in Canada has announced its intention to de-regulate and "privatize" Canadian industry as much as possible. Part of its program is the sale of

several Crown corporations to private investors. One of the first actions in this program was the sale, in early 1986, of the deHavilland company, a Crown corporation, to Boeing of the U.S. Despite heavy opposition, the government demonstrated its commitment to privatization by proceeding with and concluding the sale.

10. Based on personal communication with company executives; also see *The Citizen* 15-09-1981.

11. The publication "Commodity Trade by Industrial Sector with EEC (10)", which was made available in late 1985 by the Department of Regional Industrial Expansion, is a good example of the types of data that are needed.

12. Along these lines, in early 1986 the Canadian government indicated that it is prepared to provide financial and other support to Canadian firms wishing to participate in Eureka, the European Community's space research program. Some experts suggest that this and other similar "openings" to Europe (some of which were highlighted above) are "typical counterweight reactions" to the forthcoming Canada-U.S. free trade negotiations. Of course, only time can tell whether this is indeed the case, or whether such overtures toward EC (and other West European) countries reflect a long-term commitment to the stated goal of improving relations with all of Canada's major trading partners.

References

---

1. Main Statistical Sources

Department of Regional Industrial Expansion: *Manufacturing Trade and Measures 1966-1984*; Ottawa, 1985.

Department of Regional Industrial Expansion: *Manufacturing Trade and Measures 1966-1982*; Ottawa, 1983.

Department of Regional Industrial Expansion: *Commodity Trade by Industrial Sector with EEC (10)*; Ottawa, 1985.

European Free Trade Association: *EFTA Trade*; March 1985 (annual).

Commission of the European Communities: *Euro-Barometer* (semi-annual).

European Community: EUROSTAT - *Basic Statistics of the Community* (annual).

European Community: EUROSTAT - *Monthly External Trade Bulletin*.

International Monetary Fund: *Direction of Trade Statistics* (annual).

Organization for Economic Co-operation and Development: *Foreign Trade by Commodities* (annual).

OECD: *Main Economic Indicators (monthly)*.

OECD: *Main Economic Indicators - Historical Statistics 1964-1983.*

OECD: *International Investment and MNCs* (1981).

Statistics Canada: *Exports - Merchandise Trade (annual).*

Statistics Canada: *Imports - Merchandise Trade (annual).*

Statistics Canada: *Review of Foreign Trade 1966-1972.*

United Nations Centre on Transnational Corporations: *Transnational Corporations and International Trade: Selected Issues* (New York 1985).

UN Centre on TNCs: *Salient Features and Trends in Foreign Direct Investment* (New York 1983).

2. Bibliography

Abdel-Malek, T. (1983), "Canada's Direct Investment in Europe"; *Research Report* (mimeo), University of Calgary.

Aerospace Canada (1985), "International Cooperation in Defence Technology"; Special Supplement to *Maclean's* (November 4), SR1-16.

Anderson, E.V. (1972), "Huge European Trade Bloc Taking Shape"; *Chemical and Engineering News* (August 7) 16-17.

Anderson, P. (1981), "Vital Decisions Loom on Import Policy"; *Financial Post* (August 22) 9.

Astwood, D.M. (1981), "Canada's Merchandise Trade Record and International Competitiveness in Manufacturing, 1960 to 1979"; in Dhawan, Etemad, and Wright, *op. cit.*, 48-73.

Baker, J.C. and J.K. Ryans, Jr. (1972), "Multinational Executives Look at the European Economic Community"; *California Management Review* (Fall) 6-9.

Ball, R. (1976), "Europe: Worried But on the Mend"; *Fortune* (August) 120-125.

Banner, D.K. (1979), *Business and Society: Canadian Issues*; (Toronto: McGraw-Hill Ryerson).

Barrows, D. and P. Lyman (1975), "Foreign Ownership and Corporate Behavior in Canada"; *MSU Business Topics* (Spring) 13-20.

Barry, D. (1985), "The Canada-European Community Long Term Fisheries Agreement: Internal Politics and Fisheries Diplomacy"; *Journal of European Integration* (Fall) 5-28.

Beamish, P.W., A. Goerzen and H. Munro (1984), "The Export Characteristics of Canadian Manufacturers: A Profile by Firm Size"; *Working Paper Series* No. 8284, Department of Business, Wilfrid Laurier University.

Beckman, C.C. (1982), "Canada's International Trade Performance: A Survey of Recent Trends"; *Executive Bulletin* (Ottawa, Ont.: The Conference Board of Canada).

Beckman, C.C. (1984), *The Foreign Investment Review Agency: Images and Realities*; (Ottawa, Ont.: The Conference Board of Canada).

Bocker, H.J. and J.K.C. Toon (1984), "Some Robot Related Developments in Japan, the United States, Canada and the European Economic Community - A Comparative Analysis"; *Working Paper Series* No. 7884, Department of Business, Wilfrid Laurier University.

Britton, J.N.H. and J.M. Gilmour (1978), *The Weakest Link: A Technological Perspective on Canadian Industrial Underdevelopment*; Science Council of Canada.

Business International (1983), *Competitive Strategies for Europe*; (July).

Business Week (1966), "Three Europes, One Boom"; (September 10).

Canada's Trade Challenge: Report of the Special Committee on a National Trading Corporation (1981); House of Commons, Canada.

Canadian Economy, The (1983); *Saturday Night* and *The Conference Board of Canada* (annual report) 24-32.

Citizen, The (15-09-1981), "European Law A Boon for Local Firm"; (Ottawa) 28.

_____ (2-11-1981), "Export Aid Plan Off to Slow Start", 30.

_____ (23-12-1981), "Engineering Shortage Critical".

_____ (15-01-1985), "Survey Changes Help Close Competitive Gap".

_____ (15-05-1985), "Canada Lacks Trained Researchers", A3.

_____ (30-05-1985), "Macdonald Inquiry to Push Free Trade: Dissenting Report".

_____ (25-01-1986), "Government Deals Sweeten Canadair's Pot", A3.

_____ (21-02-1986), "Mulroney Quells Europeans' Trade Fears", A4.

The Right Honourable Joe Clark (1985), *Competitiveness and Security: Directions for Canada's International Relations*; (Ottawa, Ont.: Ministry of Supply and Services).

Cohn, T. (1978), "Canada and the EEC's Common Agricultural Policy: The Issue of Trade in Cheese"; *Journal of European Integration* (January).

Conference Board in Europe, The (1980), "Interdependence in East-West Trade"; *Economic Road Maps* (June) No. EM-1.

Cracco, E. and G. Robert (1975), "The Uncommon Common Market"; *American Marketing Association Combined Proceedings 1974*, ed. by R.C. Curhan (Chicago, Ill.: AMA) 661-667.

Crookell, H. (1985), "Fortress Canada In An Interdependent World"; *Business Quarterly* (Spring) 102-107.

Crookell, H. and J. Caliendo (1980), "International Competitiveness and the Structure of Secondary Industry in Canada"; *Business Quarterly* (Autumn) 58-64.

Dagenais, C.A. (1981), "Canada's Consulting Engineers: Prime Exporters of Technology, Goods, and Equipment"; in Dhawan, Etemad, and Wright, *op. cit.*, 220-227.

Daly, D.J. (1981a), "Canada's Comparative advantage: Implications for Industrial Strategy"; in Dhawan, Etemad, and Wright, *op. cit.*, 688-705.

_____ (1981b), "The Exporting Environment"; *Developing New Export Markets*, ed. by C.C. Beckman (Ottawa, Ont.: The Conference Board of Canada) 2-14.

_____ (1982), "Canada in an Uncertain World Economic Environment"; *Essays in International Economics* (Montreal, P.Q.: The Institute for Research on Public Policy).

Davies, C. (1983), "The View From the Womb"; *Canadian Business* (January) 48-49.

Deeg, F. (1985), "Canadian Direct Investment Abroad"; internal document, unpublished, Delegation of the Commission of the EC in Ottawa.

Dewhirst, G.H. (1981), "The Foreign Investment Review Act"; in Dhawan, Etemad and Wright, *op. cit.*, 450-465.

Diebold, W. (1968), "World Business Forum: The EEC – How Successful? How Contagious?"; *Columbia Journal of World Business* (January-February) 77-83.

Dhawan, K.C., H. Etemad, and R.W. Wright, eds., (1981), *International Business: A Canadian Perspective*, (Don Mills, Ont.: Addison-Wesley).

Dolan, M.B. (1978), "Western Europe as a Counterweight: An Analysis of Canadian-European Foreign Policy Behaviour in the Post-War Era"; *Canada's Foreign Policy: Analysis and Trends*; ed. by B. Tomlin (Toronto: Methuen) 26-50.

EC News (1985), "Baby Seals: Saved Until 1989"; Delegation of the Commission of the EC in Australia (October) 5.

Economic Council of Canada (1983), *The Bottom Line: Technology, Trade, and Income Growth*; (Ottawa, Ont.: Ministry of Supply and Services).

"EEC Expansion Offers Chance for Canada; It Reacts Slowly" (1973), *Advertising Age* (June 4) 26.

European File (1980a), Europe and the New Information Technology; Commission of the European Communities (March).

European File (1980b), Micro-Electronics and Employment; Commission of the European Communities (October).

"Europeans and the ECU" (1985); *The European Omnibus Survey* (Brussels: Gallup International).

Feld, W.J. (1984), "The CMEA and the European Community: A Troubled Courtship"; *Journal of European Integration* (Winter/Spring) 197-219.

Financial Post, The (1984), "The Financial Post 500"; (Summer) 69-160.

Forbes (1980), "Industry's Duty Free Shop"; (September 15) ;97-98.

Franko, L.G. (1978), "Multinationals: The End of U.S. Dominance"; *Harvard Business Review* (December) 93-101.

Gherson, J., G. Grattan and C.H. McMillan (1981), "Foreign Investment in Canada: An Overview by Source"; in Dhawan, Etemad, and Wright, *op. cit.*, 302-334.

Globe and Mail, The, (27-05-1985), "Report on the European Community"; R1-R8.

_____ (21-01-1986), "Canadian-made TV Throws Open Door to European Market"; A12.

Green, R.T. and A.W. Allaway (1985), "Identification of Export Opportunities: The Shift-share Approach"; *Journal of Marketing* (Winter) 83-86.

Grubel, H. (1983), *Free Market Zones: Deregulating Canadian Enterprise*; (Vancouver, B.C.: Fraser Institute).

Gwyn, R. (1981), *The Northern Magus*; (Markham, Ont.: PaperJacks).

Hay, K.A.J. (1984), "Can Canada Sustain A High-Tech Industry?"; *Business Quarterly* (Fall) 52-59.

Henry, D. (1981), Management Consultant, as quoted in *The Citizen* (5-09-1981): "Canadians Hesitant Children in World Markets: Economist"; (Ottawa) 48.

Heslop, L.A. and M. Wall (1985), "Differences Between Men and Women in the Formation of Country of Origin Product Images"; in J.C. Chebat, ed., *Marketing* (Montreal: Proceedings of the Administrative Sciences Association of Canada, Marketing Division) 148-157.

Houston, M. and S. Sudman (1975), "A Methodological Assessment of the Use of Key Informants"; *Social Science Research* (4) 151-164.

Hudson, R., D. Rhind and H. Mounsey (1984), *An Atlas of EEC Affairs*; (London, U.K.: Methuen).

Huff, D.L. and L.A. Scherr (1967), "A Measure for Determining Differential Growth Rates of Markets"; *Journal of Marketing Research* (November) 391-395.

Hurtig, M. (1979), "Canada on a Platter"; *Canadian Business* (July).

International Business Perspectives (1986), "Canada's Trade Surplus Still Shrinking", and "Canada Has Top Revenue Share From Foreign Investment in the United States"; The Conference Board of Canada (January) 1-2.

Jayawardena, D.L.U. (1983), "Free Trade Zones"; *Journal of World Trade Law* (September-October) 427-444.

Jenkins, M. (1981), Science Adviser, Science Council of Canada, as quoted in *The Citizen* (26-11-1981): "Act Now to Save Hi-Tech Industry, Report Tells Government"; (Ottawa) 35.

Jones, V.J. (1986), "International Marketing of Services: A Canadian Perspective"; in *International Marketing Strategy: Proceedings of a Workshop*, ed. by F.M. Bradley and N.G. Papadopoulos (Brussels: The European Institute for Advanced Studies in Management) 92-101.

Journal of Commerce (1983), Special Issue on Free Trade Zones; (November 8).

Kaynak, E. (1981), "Internationalization of Nova Scotia Manufacturing Firms: Exporters Versus Non-Exporters"; *Research Report* (mimeo), Mount Saint Vincent University, Halifax, Nova Scotia.

The Honourable James Kelleher (1986), "The Importance of Britain and Europe in Canada's Trade Strategy"; *Luncheon Address*, Canada's High Commission in London and the Canada-U.K. Chamber of Commerce (February 10).

Kirpalani, V. (1985), *International Marketing*; (New York, N.Y.: Random House).

Kotler, P., L. Fahey and S. Jatusripitak (1985), *The New Competition*; (Englewood Cliffs, N.J.: Prentice-Hall).

Kransdorff, A. (1984), "Multinationals and European Integration: A Lack of European Harmony"; *Multinational Info*, Institut de Recherche et d'Information sur les Multinationales (June) 2-5.

Kravis, I.B. (1962), "Common Market — Lesson in Trade Expansion"; *Harvard Business Review* (March-April) 6ff.

Lasvergnas-Grémy, I. (1976), *L'Europe vue du Canada*; (Montréal, P.Q.: Centre de Sondage et Centre d'Études et de Documentation Européennes, Université de Montréal).

LeDuc, L. and J.A. Murray (1984), "Public Opinion and North American Integration: Pragmatic Nationalism"; *The Integration Question: Political Economy and Public Policy in Canada and North America*; ed. by J.H. Pammett and B. Tomlin (Don Mills, Ont.: Addison-Wesley) 129-143.

Leonard, D. (1983), "China Opens Up to the EEC"; *Europe* (Winter) 11-14.

Levitt, T. (1983), *The Marketing Imagination* (London, U.K.: Collier Macmillan Publishers).

Lilley, W. (1983), "Making It In World Markets"; *Canadian Business* (January) 28-29.

Litvak, I.A. (1984), *Canadian Cases in International Business*; (Toronto, Ont.: McGraw-Hill Ryerson).

_____ and C.J. Maule (1981), *The Canadian Multinationals*; (Toronto, Ont.: Butterworth).

Lugon, J. (1985), "EFTA-EC Cooperation: From 'Yesterday' to 'Tomorrow'"; *EFTA Bulletin* (No. 1/85).

Lukasiewicz, M. (1981), "The Third Option Becomes an Embarrassment as Canada's Hopes for More Trade Founder"; *The Globe and Mail*, Special Report on the EEC (September 14).

Macdonald Royal Commission (1985), *Report of the Royal Commission on the Economic Union and Development Prospects in Canada*, D.S. Macdonald, Chairman (Ottawa: Supply and Services), Vol. I, II, and III.

McEvoy, H.S. (1975), "The Real Impact of The Common Market: The Multi-National"; *American Marketing Association Combined Proceedings 1974*, ed. by R.C. Curhan (Chicago, Ill.: AMA) 668-670.

Morrice, J. (1985), "Three Cheers for Lomé III"; *Europe* (Spring) 12-17.

Munton, D. and D. Swanson (1978), "Rise and Fall of the Third Option: Forecasting Canadian-American Relations into the 1980s"; *Canada's Foreign Policy: Analysis and Trends*; ed. by B. Tomlin (Toronto, Ont.: Methuen) 175-213.

Nadeau, B. (1985), *Britain's Entry into the European Economic Community and its Effect on Canada's Agricultural Exports*; Essays in International Economics (Montreal, P.Q.: The Institute for Research on Public Policy).

Norvell, D.G. and S. Raveed (1980), "Eleven Reasons for Firms to 'Go International'"; *Marketing News* (October 17) 1-2.

The Honourable Frank Oberle (1986), "Canadian Government
Policy and the Development of High Technology Industry";
Address to the Conference *Managing High Technology:
Decisions for Success,* The Research Centre for High
Technology Management, Carleton University (February
27).

OECD Economic Surveys: Canada (1984); (Paris, France:
OECD).

Papadopoulos, N.G. (1982a), "Internationalizing Canadian
Business: Problems and Opportunities in the European
Economic Community"; *Research Report* (mimeo); (London,
Ont.: Associates' Workshop in Business Research,
University of Western Ontario).

_____ (1982b), "The European Economic Community: One
Market, Ten Markets — or Twelve?"; *Developments in
Marketing Science,* ed. by V. Kothari (Nacogdoches, Texas:
Academy of Marketing Science) 215-220.

_____ (1982c), "The European Economic Community as a
Potential Market for Canadian Goods"; *The Future: Today's
Challenge* (Ottawa, Ont.: Administrative Sciences
Association of Canada) 219-228.

_____ (1985), "The Free Trade Zone as a Strategic Element in
International Business"; *Canadian Business Review* (Spring)
51-55.

_____ and J. Berács (1985), "Expanding the Scope of Research
to Eastern Shortage Economies"; *Broadening the Uses of
Research,* 38th ESOMAR Congress (Amsterdam, The
Netherlands: European Society for Opinion and Marketing
Research) 1-20.

_____ and L.A. Heslop (1986), "Travel as a Correlate of Product
and Country Images"; in T. Muller, ed., *Marketing* (Whistler,
B.C.: Administrative Sciences Association of Canada,
Marketing Division) 191-200.

_____, L.A. Heslop, F. Graby, and G. Avlonitis (1986), "A
Cross-National View of Consumer Predispositions Toward
Products from Foreign Countries"; in *Anticipation and
Decision Making: The Need for Information,* 39th ESOMAR

Congress (Amsterdam, The Netherlands: European Society for Opinion and Marketing Research) 91-117.

Pelkmans, J. (1983), "European Direct Investments in the European Community"; *Journal of European Integration* (Fall) 41-70.

Phillips, L.W. (1980), *On Studying Collective Behavior: Methodological Issues in the Use of Key Informants*; unpublished Ph.D. dissertation, Northwestern University.

Reisman, S.S. (1984), "The Issue of Free Trade"; in *U.S.-Canadian Economic Relations: Next Steps?*, ed. by E.R. Fried and P.H. Trezise (Washington, D.C.: The Brookings Institution) 35-51.

Rostein, A. (1976), "Canada: The New Nationalism"; *Foreign Affairs* (October) 97-118.

Rugman, A.M. (1983), "Multinational Enterprises and World Product Mandates"; *Multinationals and Technology Transfer: The Canadian Experience*, ed. by A.M. Rugman (New York, N.Y.: Praeger).

_____ (1985), "The Marketing Advantages of Canadian Multinationals"; *International Business* - Proceedings of the 1985 Conference of the Administrative Sciences Association of Canada; 143-152.

_____ and J. McIlveen (1984), "Canadian Multinationals: Identification, Performance, and Strategic Management"; *Dalhousie Discussion Papers in International Business*, No. 39 (Halifax, Nova Scotia: Dalhousie University).

Rutenberg, D. (1981), "Global Product Mandating"; in Dhawan, Etemad, and Wright, *op. cit.*, 588-598.

Safarian, A.E. (1981), "Some Myths About Foreign Business Investment"; *Journal of Canadian Studies* (August).

Salehizadeh, M. (1983), "Regulations of Foreign Direct Investment by Host Countries"; *Essays in International Business*, Center for International Business Studies, The University of South Carolina (May).

Sampson, A. (1985), *Empires of the Sky* (London, U.K.: Hodder and Stoughton).

Science Council of Canada (1971), *Innovation in a Cold Climate: The Dilemma of Canadian Manufacturing*; (Ottawa; October).

_____ (1981), *Hard Times, Hard Choices*; (Ottawa).

_____ (1984), *Canadian Industrial Development: Some Policy Directions*; (Ottawa).

Scrivener, R.C. (1979), "International Markets or Die"; *Business Quarterly* (Summer) 72-75.

Sharp, M. (1972), "Canadian-U.S. Relations"; *International Perspectives* (Autumn) 13-23.

Spain and the EEC (1986); Financial Times Survey, *Financial Times* (January 20) 1ff.

Stone, F. (1984), *Canada, the GATT and the International Trade System*; Essays in International Economics (Montreal, P.Q.: The Institute for Research on Public Policy).

Survey of Multinational Enterprises (1976); Commission of the European Communities (Brussels; July).

Sweeney, T. (1980), "Sound the Alert to Canadian Industrialists: The Tokyo Round of Trade Negotiations"; *Business Quarterly* (Summer) 83-86.

Ting, W. (1980), "New Wave Multinationals"; *Marketing News* (October 17) 12.

Twaalfhoven, B. (1978), "Foreign Investment Review Act: Comments by a Concerned Dutch Party"; *Business Quarterly* (Spring).

UNCTAD - United Nations Conference on Trade and Development (1983), "Export Processing Free Zones in Developing Countries"; *Doc. No. TD/B/C.2/211* (January 18).

von Franque, V. (1986), President and C.E.O., The Dresdner Bank of Canada; Seminar Address, *Foreign Investment in Canada:*

A Foreign Banker's View and Experience; The International Business Study Group, Carleton University (February).

von Riekhoff, H. (1978), "The Third Option in Canadian Foreign Policy"; in *Canada's Foreign Policy: Analysis and Trends*; ed. by B. Tomlin (Toronto, Ont.: Methuen) 87-109.

_____ and B. Tomlin (1984), "The Politics of Interdependence: Canada-United States Intergovernmental Relations"; in *The Integration Question: Political Economy and Public Policy in Canada and North America*; ed. by J.H. Pammett and B. Tomlin (Don Mills, Ont.: Addison-Wesley) 144-162.

Voyer, R.D. and M.G. Murphy (1984), *Global 2000: Canada - A View of Canadian Economic Development Prospects, Resources and the Environment*; (Toronto, Ont.: Pergamon Press).

Welch, L.S. and F. Wiedersheim-Paul (1980), "Initial Exports — A Marketing Failure?"; *Journal of Management Studies* (October) 333-344.

Witten, M. (1981), "Taking Care of Business"; *Saturday Night* (November) 15-16.

Wright, R.W. (1981), "Turnkey Projects: Canada's Route to Third World Markets"; in Dhawan, Etemad, and Wright, *op. cit.*, 506-522.

_____ (1984), *Japanese Business in Canada: The Elusive Alliance*; Essays in International Economics (Montreal, P.Q.: Institute for Research on Public Policy).

The Members of the Institute

125

Dr. K. George Pedersen
President, University of Western
Ontario, London
Professor Marilyn L. Pilkington
Osgoode Hall Law School, Toronto
Dr. Stuart L. Smith
Canada, Ottawa
Eldon D. Thompson
Chairman Science Council of
President, Telesat, Vanier
Dr. Israel Unger
Deean of Science
University of New Brunswick
Fredericton
Philip Vineberg, O.C., Q.C.
Phillips & Vineberg, Montreal
Dr. Norman Wagner
President and Vice-Chancellor
University of Calgary
Ida Wasacase, C.M.
Winnipeg
Mr. Ronald L. Watts
Department of Political Studies
Queen's University, Kingston
Dr. R. Sherman Weaver
Director, Alberta Environmental
Centre, Vegreville
Dr. Blossom Wigdor
Director, Program in Gerontology
University of Toronto

Government Representatives
Herb Clarke, Newfoundland
Joseph H. Clarke, Nova Scotia
George Ford, Manitoba
George de Rappard, Alberta
Hershell Ezrin, Ontario
Honourable Lowell Murray, Canada
John H. Parker, Northwest Territories
Roger Burke, Prince Edward Island
Norman Riddell, Saskatchewan
Christian Dufour, Québec
Norman Spector, British Columbia
Eloise Spitzer, Yukon
Barry Toole, New Brunswick

Institute Management

Rod Dobell	President
Peter Dobell	Vice-President and Secretary-Treasurer
Yvon Gasse	Director, Small & Medium-Sized Business Program
Barbara L. Hodgins	Director, Western Resources Program
John Langford	Director, Governability Research Program
Barry Lesser	Director, Information Society Studies Program
Shirley Seward	Director, Studies in Social Policy
Frank Stone	Director, International Economics Program
Parker Staples	Director, Financial Services
Donald Wilson	Director, Communications
Louis Vagianos	Director, Publishing Services
Tom Kent	Editor, *Policy Options Politiques*

Fellows- and Scholars-in-Residence:

Edgar Gallant	Fellow-in-Residence
Tom Kent	Fellow-in-Residence
Eric Kierans	Fellow-in-Residence
Jean-Luc Pepin	Fellow-in-Residence
Gordon Robertson	Fellow-in-Residence
Richard Brown	Scholar-in-Residence

Publications Available - Sept. 1986

Order Address:
The Institute for Research on Public Policy
P.O. Box 3670 South
Halifax, Nova Scotia
B3J 3K6

Leroy O. Stone & Claude Marceau	*Canadian Population Trends and Public Policy Through the 1980s.* 1977 $4.00
Raymond Breton	*The Canadian Condition: A Guide to Research in Public Policy.* 1977 $2.95
Raymond Breton	*Une orientation de la recherche politique dans le contexte canadien.* 1977 $2.95
J.W. Rowley & W.T. Stanbury (eds.)	*Competition Policy in Canada: Stage II, Bill C-13.* 1978 $12.95
C.F. Smart & W.T. Stanbury (eds.)	*Studies on Crisis Management.* 1978 $9.95
W.T. Stanbury (ed.)	*Studies on Regulation in Canada.* 1978 $9.95
Michael Hudson	*Canada in the New Monetary Order: Borrow? Devalue? Restructure!* 1978 $6.95
David K. Foot (ed.)	*Public Employment and Compensation in Canada: Myths and Realities.* 1978 $10.95
Raymond Breton & Gail Grant Akian	*Urban Institutions and People of Indian Ancestry: Suggestions for Research.* 1979 $3.00
Thomas H. Atkinson	*Trends in Life Satisfaction Among Canadians, 1968-1977.* 1979 $3.00
W.E. Cundiff & Mado Reid (eds.)	*Issues in Canadian/U.S. Transborder Computer Data Flows.* 1979 $6.50
Meyer W. Bucovetsky (ed.)	*Studies in Public Employment and Compensation in Canada.* 1979 $14.95

131

Richard French & André Béliveau	*The RCMP and the Management of National Security.* 1979 $6.95
Richard French & André Béliveau	*La GRC et la gestion de la sécurité nationale.* 1979 $6.95
G. Bruce Doern & Allan M. Maslove (eds.)	*The Public Evaluation of Government Spending.* 1979 $10.95
Leroy O. Stone & Michael J. MacLean	*Future Income Prospects for Canada's Senior Citizens.* 1979 $7.95
Richard M. Bird	*The Growth of Public Employment in Canada.* 1979 $12.95
Richard J. Schultz	*Federalism and the Regulatory Process.* 1979 $1.50
Richard J. Schultz	*Le fédéralisme et le processus de réglementation.* 1979 $1.50
Lionel D. Feldman & Katherine A. Graham	*Bargaining for Cities, Municipalities and Intergovernmental Relations: An Assessment.* 1979 $10.95
Elliot J. Feldman & Neil Nevitte (eds.)	*The Future of North America: Canada, the United States, and Quebec Nationalism.* 1979 $7.95
David R. Protheroe	*Imports and Politics: Trade Decision Making in Canada, 1968-1979.* 1980 $8.95
G. Bruce Doern	*Government Intervention in the Canadian Nuclear Industry.* 1980 $8.95
G. Bruce Doern & Robert W. Morrison (eds.)	*Canadian Nuclear Policies.* 1980 $14.95
Allan M. Maslove & Gene Swimmer	*Wage Controls in Canada: 1975-78: A Study of Public Decision Making.* 1980 $11.95
T. Gregory Kane	*Consumers and the Regulators: Intervention in the Federal Regulatory Process.* 1980 $10.95
Réjean Lachapelle & Jacques Henripin	*La situation démolinguistique au Canada: évolution passée et prospective.* 1980 $24.95
Albert Breton & Anthony Scott	*The Design of Federations.* 1980 $6.95
A.R. Bailey & D.G. Hull	*The Way Out: A More Revenue-Dependent Public Sector and How It Might Revitalize the Process of Governing.* 1980 $6.95
David R. Harvey	*Christmas Turkey or Prairie Vulture? An Economic Analysis of the Crow's Nest Pass Grain Rates.* 1980 $10.95
Donald G. Cartwright	*Official Language Populations in Canada: Patterns and Contacts.* 1980 $4.95
Richard M. Bird	*Taxing Corporations.* 1980 $6.95

Leroy O. Stone & Susan Fletcher	*A Profile of Canada's Older Population.* 1980 $7.95
Peter N. Nemetz (ed.)	*Resource Policy: International Perspectives.* 1980 $18.95
Keith A.J. Hay (ed.)	*Canadian Perspectives on Economic Relations* *With Japan.* 1980 $18.95
Dhiru Patel	*Dealing With Interracial Conflict: Policy* *Alternatives.* 1980 $5.95
Raymond Breton & Gail Grant	*La langue de travail au Québec : synthèse de la* *recherche sur la rencontre de deux langues.* 1981 $10.95
Diane Vanasse	*L'évolution de la population scolaire du Québec.* 1981 $12.95
David M. Cameron (ed.)	*Regionalism and Supranationalism:* *Challenges and Alternatives to the Nation-State* *in Canada and Europe.* 1981 $9.95
Heather Menzies	*Women and the Chip: Case Studies of the* *Effects of Information on Employment in* *Canada.* 1981 $8.95
H.V. Kroeker (ed.)	*Sovereign People or Sovereign Governments.* 1981 $12.95
Peter Aucoin (ed.)	*The Politics and Management of Restraint in* *Government.* 1981 $17.95
Nicole S. Morgan	*Nowhere to Go? Possible Consequences of the* *Demographic Imbalance in Decision-Making* *Groups of the Federal Public Service.* 1981 $8.95
Nicole S. Morgan	*Où aller? Les conséquences prévisibles des* *déséquilibres démographiques chez les groupes* *de décision de la fonction publique fédérale.* 1981 $8.95
Raymond Breton, Jeffrey G. Reitz & Victor F. Valentine	*Les frontières culturelles et la cohésion du* *Canada.* 1981 $18.95
Peter N. Nemetz (ed.)	*Energy Crisis: Policy Response.* 1981 $10.95
James Gillies	*Where Business Fails.* 1981 $9.95
Allan Tupper & G. Bruce Doern (eds.)	*Public Corporations and Public Policy in* *Canada.* 1981 $16.95
Réjean Lachapelle & Jacques Henripin	*The Demolinguistic Situation in Canada: Past* *Trends and Future Prospects.* 1982 $24.95
Irving Brecher	*Canada's Competition Policy Revisited: Some* *New Thoughts on an Old Story.* 1982 $3.00
Ian McAllister	*Regional Development and the European* *Community: A Canadian Perspective.* 1982 $13.95

Donald J. Daly	*Canada in an Uncertain World Economic Environment.* 1982 $3.00
W.T. Stanbury & Fred Thompson	*Regulatory Reform in Canada.* 1982 $7.95
Robert J. Buchan, C. Christopher Johnston, T. Gregory Kane, Barry Lesser, Richard J. Schultz & W.T. Stanbury	*Telecommunications Regulation and the Constitution.* 1982 $18.95
Rodney de C. Grey	*United States Trade Policy Legislation: A Canadian View.* 1982 $7.95
John Quinn & Philip Slayton (eds.)	*Non-Tariff Barriers After the Tokyo Round.* 1982 $17.95
Stanley M. Beck & Ivan Bernier (eds.)	*Canada and the New Constitution: The Unfinished Agenda.* 2 vols. 1983 $10.95 (set)
R. Brian Woodrow & Kenneth B. Woodside (eds.)	*The Introduction of Pay-TV in Canada: Issues and Implications.* 1983 $14.95
E.P. Weeks & L. Mazany	*The Future of the Atlantic Fisheries.* 1983 $5.00
Douglas D. Purvis (ed.), assisted by Frances Chambers	*The Canadian Balance of Payments: Perspectives and Policy Issues.* 1983 $24.95
Roy A. Matthews	*Canada and the "Little Dragons": An Analysis of Economic Developments in Hong Kong, Taiwan, and South Korea and the Challenge/ Opportunity They Present for Canadian Interests in the 1980s.* 1983 $11.95
Charles Pearson & Gerry Salembier	*Trade, Employment, and Adjustment.* 1983 $5.00
Steven Globerman	*Cultural Regulation in Canada.* 1983 $11.95
F.R. Flatters & R.G. Lipsey	*Common Ground for the Canadian Common Market.* 1983 $5.00
Frank Bunn, assisted by U. Domb, D. Huntley, H. Mills, H. Silverstein	*Oceans from Space: Towards the Management of Our Coastal Zones.* 1983 $5.00
C.D. Shearing & P.C. Stenning	*Private Security and Private Justice: The Challenge of the 80s.* 1983 $5.00
Jacob Finkelman & Shirley B. Goldenberg	*Collective Bargaining in the Public Service: The Federal Experience in Canada.* 2 vols. 1983 $29.95 (set)
Gail Grant	*The Concrete Reserve: Corporate Programs for Indians in the Urban Work Place.* 1983 $5.00
Owen Adams & Russell Wilkins	*Healthfulness of Life.* 1983 $8.00

Yoshi Tsurumi with Rebecca R. Tsurumi	*Sogoshosha: Engines of Export-Based Growth.* (Revised Edition). 1984 $10.95
Raymond Breton & Gail Grant (eds.)	*The Dynamics of Government Programs for Urban Indians in the Prairie Provinces.* 1984 $19.95
Frank Stone	*Canada, The GATT and the International Trade System.* 1984 $15.00
Pierre Sauvé	*Private Bank Lending and Developing-Country Debt.* 1984 $10.00
Mark Thompson & Gene Swimmer	*Conflict or Compromise: The Future of Public Sector Industrial Relations.* 1984 $15.00
Samuel Wex	*Instead of FIRA: Autonomy for Canadian Subsidiaries?* 1984 $8.00
R.J. Wonnacott	*Selected New Developments in International Trade Theory.* 1984 $7.00
R.J. Wonnacott	*Aggressive US Reciprocity Evaluated with a New Analytical Approach to Trade Conflicts.* 1984 $8.00
Richard W. Wright	*Japanese Business in Canada: The Elusive Alliance.* 1984 $12.00
Paul K. Gorecki & W.T. Stanbury	*The Objectives of Canadian Competition Policy, 1888-1983.* 1984 $15.00
Michael Hart	*Some Thoughts on Canada-United States Sectoral Free Trade.* 1985 $7.00
J. Peter Meekison Roy J. Romanow & William D. Moull	*Origins and Meaning of Section 92A: The 1982 Constitutional Amendment on Resources.* 1985 $10.00
Conference Papers	*Canada and International Trade. Volume One: Major Issues of Canadian Trade Policy. Volume Two: Canada and the Pacific Rim.* 1985 $25.00 (set)
A.E. Safarian	*Foreign Direct Investment: A Survey of Canadian Research.* 1985 $8.00
Joseph R. D'Cruz & James D. Fleck	*Canada Can Compete! Strategic Management of the Canadian Industrial Portfolio.* 1985 $18.00
Barry Lesser & Louis Vagianos	*Computer Communications and the Mass Market in Canada.* 1985 $10.00
W.R. Hines	*Trade Policy Making in Canada: Are We Doing it Right?* 1985 $10.00
Bertrand Nadeau	*Britain's Entry into the European Economic Community and its Effect on Canada's Agricultural Exports.* 1985 $10.00

Paul B. Huber	*Promoting Timber Cropping: Policies Toward Non-Industrial Forest Owners in New Brunswick.* 1985 $10.00
Gordon Robertson	*Northern Provinces: A Mistaken Goal.* *1985* $8.00
Petr Hanel	*La technologie et les exportations canadiennes du matériel pour la filière bois-papier.* 1985 $20.00
Russel M. Wills, Steven Globerman & Peter J. Booth	*Software Policies for Growth and Export.* 1986 $15.00
Marc Malone	*Une place pour le Québec au Canada.* 1986 $20.00
A. R. Dobell & S. H. Mansbridge	*The Social Policy Process in Canada.* 1986 $8.00
William D. Shipman (ed.)	*Trade and Investment Across the Northeast Boundary: Quebec, the Atlantic Provinces, and New England.* 1986 $20.00
Nicole Morgan	*Implosion: An Analysis of the Growth of the Federal Public Service in Canada (1945-1985).* 1986 $20.00
Nicole Morgan	*Implosion: analyse de la croissance de la Fonction publique fédérale canadienne (1945-1985).* 1986 $20.00
William A.W. Neilson & Chad Gaffield (eds.)	*Universities in Crisis: A Mediaeval Institution in the Twenty-first Century.* 1986 $20.00
Fred Wien	*Rebuilding the Economic Base of Indian Communities: The Micmac in Nova Scotia.* 1986 $20.00
D.M. Daly & D.C. MacCharles	*Canadian Manufactured Exports: Constraints and Opportunities.* 1986 $20.00
Gerald d'Amboise, Yvon Gasse & Rob Dainow	*The Smaller, Independent Manufacturer: 12 Quebec Case Studies.* 1986 $20.00
David J. Roy & Maurice A.M. de Wachter	*The Life Technologies and Public Policy.* 1986 $20.00
David Feeny, Gordon Guyatt & Peter Tugwell (eds.)	*Health Care Technology: Effectiveness, Efficiency, and Public Policy.* 1986 $20.00
International Symposium	*Les répercussions de l'informatisation en milieu de travail / The Impact of New Information Technologies on the Workplace.* 1986 $20.00
N.G. Papadopoulos	*Canada and the European Community: An Uncomfortable Partnership?* 1986 $15.00